Mometrix
TEST PREPARATION

Secrets of the

CPIM®

Master Planning of Resources Exam Study Guide

Dear Future Exam Success Story

First of all, **THANK YOU** for purchasing Mometrix study materials!

Second, congratulations! You are one of the few determined test-takers who are committed to doing whatever it takes to excel on your exam. **You have come to the right place.** We developed these study materials with one goal in mind: to deliver you the information you need in a format that's concise and easy to use.

In addition to optimizing your guide for the content of the test, we've outlined our recommended steps for breaking down the preparation process into small, attainable goals so you can make sure you stay on track.

We've also analyzed the entire test-taking process, identifying the most common pitfalls and showing how you can overcome them and be ready for any curveball the test throws you.

Standardized testing is one of the biggest obstacles on your road to success, which only increases the importance of doing well in the high-pressure, high-stakes environment of test day. Your results on this test could have a significant impact on your future, and this guide provides the information and practical advice to help you achieve your full potential on test day.

Your success is our success

We would love to hear from you! If you would like to share the story of your exam success or if you have any questions or comments in regard to our products, please contact us at **800-673-8175** or **support@mometrix.com**.

Thanks again for your business and we wish you continued success!

Sincerely,
The Mometrix Test Preparation Team

Need more help? Check out our flashcards at:
http://MometrixFlashcards.com/CPIM

Written and edited by the Mometrix Exam Secrets Test Prep Team
Printed in the United States of America

Table of Contents

Introduction

Thank you for purchasing this resource! You have made the choice to prepare yourself for a test that could have a huge impact on your future, and this guide is designed to help you be fully ready for test day. Obviously, it's important to have a solid understanding of the test material, but you also need to be prepared for the unique environment and stressors of the test, so that you can perform to the best of your abilities.

For this purpose, the first section that appears in this guide is the **Secret Keys**. We've devoted countless hours to meticulously researching what works and what doesn't, and we've boiled down our findings to the five most impactful steps you can take to improve your performance on the test. We start at the beginning with study planning and move through the preparation process, all the way to the testing strategies that will help you get the most out of what you know when you're finally sitting in front of the test.

We recommend that you start preparing for your test as far in advance as possible. However, if you've bought this guide as a last-minute study resource and only have a few days before your test, we recommend that you skip over the first two Secret Keys since they address a long-term study plan.

If you struggle with **test anxiety**, we strongly encourage you to check out our recommendations for how you can overcome it. Test anxiety is a formidable foe, but it can be beaten, and we want to make sure you have the tools you need to defeat it.

Secret Key #1 – Plan Big, Study Small

There's a lot riding on your performance. If you want to ace this test, you're going to need to keep your skills sharp and the material fresh in your mind. You need a plan that lets you review everything you need to know while still fitting in your schedule. We'll break this strategy down into three categories.

Information Organization

Start with the information you already have: the official test outline. From this, you can make a complete list of all the concepts you need to cover before the test. Organize these concepts into groups that can be studied together, and create a list of any related vocabulary you need to learn so you can brush up on any difficult terms. You'll want to keep this vocabulary list handy once you actually start studying since you may need to add to it along the way.

Time Management

Once you have your set of study concepts, decide how to spread them out over the time you have left before the test. Break your study plan into small, clear goals so you have a manageable task for each day and know exactly what you're doing. Then just focus on one small step at a time. When you manage your time this way, you don't need to spend hours at a time studying. Studying a small block of content for a short period each day helps you retain information better and avoid stressing over how much you have left to do. You can relax knowing that you have a plan to cover everything in time. In order for this strategy to be effective though, you have to start studying early and stick to your schedule. Avoid the exhaustion and futility that comes from last-minute cramming!

Study Environment

The environment you study in has a big impact on your learning. Studying in a coffee shop, while probably more enjoyable, is not likely to be as fruitful as studying in a quiet room. It's important to keep distractions to a minimum. You're only planning to study for a short block of time, so make the most of it. Don't pause to check your phone or get up to find a snack. It's also important to **avoid multitasking**. Research has consistently shown that multitasking will make your studying dramatically less effective. Your study area should also be comfortable and well-lit so you don't have the distraction of straining your eyes or sitting on an uncomfortable chair.

The time of day you study is also important. You want to be rested and alert. Don't wait until just before bedtime. Study when you'll be most likely to comprehend and remember. Even better, if you know what time of day your test will be, set that time aside for study. That way your brain will be used to working on that subject at that specific time and you'll have a better chance of recalling information.

Finally, it can be helpful to team up with others who are studying for the same test. Your actual studying should be done in as isolated an environment as possible, but the work of organizing the information and setting up the study plan can be divided up. In between study sessions, you can discuss with your teammates the concepts that you're all studying and quiz each other on the details. Just be sure that your teammates are as serious about the test as you are. If you find that your study time is being replaced with social time, you might need to find a new team.

Secret Key #2 – Make Your Studying Count

You're devoting a lot of time and effort to preparing for this test, so you want to be absolutely certain it will pay off. This means doing more than just reading the content and hoping you can remember it on test day. It's important to make every minute of study count. There are two main areas you can focus on to make your studying count.

Retention

It doesn't matter how much time you study if you can't remember the material. You need to make sure you are retaining the concepts. To check your retention of the information you're learning, try recalling it at later times with minimal prompting. Try carrying around flashcards and glance at one or two from time to time or ask a friend who's also studying for the test to quiz you.

To enhance your retention, look for ways to put the information into practice so that you can apply it rather than simply recalling it. If you're using the information in practical ways, it will be much easier to remember. Similarly, it helps to solidify a concept in your mind if you're not only reading it to yourself but also explaining it to someone else. Ask a friend to let you teach them about a concept you're a little shaky on (or speak aloud to an imaginary audience if necessary). As you try to summarize, define, give examples, and answer your friend's questions, you'll understand the concepts better and they will stay with you longer. Finally, step back for a big picture view and ask yourself how each piece of information fits with the whole subject. When you link the different concepts together and see them working together as a whole, it's easier to remember the individual components.

Finally, practice showing your work on any multi-step problems, even if you're just studying. Writing out each step you take to solve a problem will help solidify the process in your mind, and you'll be more likely to remember it during the test.

Modality

Modality simply refers to the means or method by which you study. Choosing a study modality that fits your own individual learning style is crucial. No two people learn best in exactly the same way, so it's important to know your strengths and use them to your advantage.

For example, if you learn best by visualization, focus on visualizing a concept in your mind and draw an image or a diagram. Try color-coding your notes, illustrating them, or creating symbols that will trigger your mind to recall a learned concept. If you learn best by hearing or discussing information, find a study partner who learns the same way or read aloud to yourself. Think about how to put the information in your own words. Imagine that you are giving a lecture on the topic and record yourself so you can listen to it later.

For any learning style, flashcards can be helpful. Organize the information so you can take advantage of spare moments to review. Underline key words or phrases. Use different colors for different categories. Mnemonic devices (such as creating a short list in which every item starts with the same letter) can also help with retention. Find what works best for you and use it to store the information in your mind most effectively and easily.

Secret Key #3 – Practice the Right Way

Your success on test day depends not only on how many hours you put into preparing, but also on whether you prepared the right way. It's good to check along the way to see if your studying is paying off. One of the most effective ways to do this is by taking practice tests to evaluate your progress. Practice tests are useful because they show exactly where you need to improve. Every time you take a practice test, pay special attention to these three groups of questions:

- The questions you got wrong
- The questions you had to guess on, even if you guessed right
- The questions you found difficult or slow to work through

This will show you exactly what your weak areas are, and where you need to devote more study time. Ask yourself why each of these questions gave you trouble. Was it because you didn't understand the material? Was it because you didn't remember the vocabulary? Do you need more repetitions on this type of question to build speed and confidence? Dig into those questions and figure out how you can strengthen your weak areas as you go back to review the material.

Additionally, many practice tests have a section explaining the answer choices. It can be tempting to read the explanation and think that you now have a good understanding of the concept. However, an explanation likely only covers part of the question's broader context. Even if the explanation makes perfect sense, **go back and investigate** every concept related to the question until you're positive you have a thorough understanding.

As you go along, keep in mind that the practice test is just that: practice. Memorizing these questions and answers will not be very helpful on the actual test because it is unlikely to have any of the same exact questions. If you only know the right answers to the sample questions, you won't be prepared for the real thing. **Study the concepts** until you understand them fully, and then you'll be able to answer any question that shows up on the test.

It's important to wait on the practice tests until you're ready. If you take a test on your first day of study, you may be overwhelmed by the amount of material covered and how much you need to learn. Work up to it gradually.

On test day, you'll need to be prepared for answering questions, managing your time, and using the test-taking strategies you've learned. It's a lot to balance, like a mental marathon that will have a big impact on your future. Like training for a marathon, you'll need to start slowly and work your way up. When test day arrives, you'll be ready.

Start with the strategies you've read in the first two Secret Keys—plan your course and study in the way that works best for you. If you have time, consider using multiple study resources to get different approaches to the same concepts. It can be helpful to see difficult concepts from more than one angle. Then find a good source for practice tests. Many times, the test website will suggest potential study resources or provide sample tests.

Practice Test Strategy

If you're able to find at least three practice tests, we recommend this strategy:

Untimed and Open-Book Practice

Take the first test with no time constraints and with your notes and study guide handy. Take your time and focus on applying the strategies you've learned.

Timed and Open-Book Practice

Take the second practice test open-book as well, but set a timer and practice pacing yourself to finish in time.

Timed and Closed-Book Practice

Take any other practice tests as if it were test day. Set a timer and put away your study materials. Sit at a table or desk in a quiet room, imagine yourself at the testing center, and answer questions as quickly and accurately as possible.

Keep repeating timed and closed-book tests on a regular basis until you run out of practice tests or it's time for the actual test. Your mind will be ready for the schedule and stress of test day, and you'll be able to focus on recalling the material you've learned.

Secret Key #4 – Pace Yourself

Once you're fully prepared for the material on the test, your biggest challenge on test day will be managing your time. Just knowing that the clock is ticking can make you panic even if you have plenty of time left. Work on pacing yourself so you can build confidence against the time constraints of the exam. Pacing is a difficult skill to master, especially in a high-pressure environment, so **practice is vital**.

Set time expectations for your pace based on how much time is available. For example, if a section has 60 questions and the time limit is 30 minutes, you know you have to average 30 seconds or less per question in order to answer them all. Although 30 seconds is the hard limit, set 25 seconds per question as your goal, so you reserve extra time to spend on harder questions. When you budget extra time for the harder questions, you no longer have any reason to stress when those questions take longer to answer.

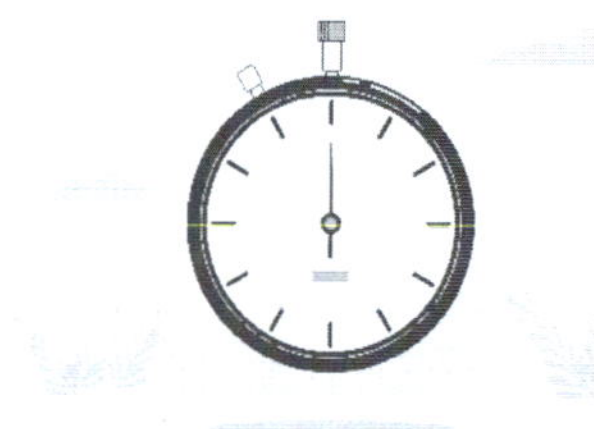

Don't let this time expectation distract you from working through the test at a calm, steady pace, but keep it in mind so you don't spend too much time on any one question. Recognize that taking extra time on one question you don't understand may keep you from answering two that you do understand later in the test. If your time limit for a question is up and you're still not sure of the answer, mark it and move on, and come back to it later if the time and the test format allow. If the testing format doesn't allow you to return to earlier questions, just make an educated guess; then put it out of your mind and move on.

On the easier questions, be careful not to rush. It may seem wise to hurry through them so you have more time for the challenging ones, but it's not worth missing one if you know the concept and just didn't take the time to read the question fully. Work efficiently but make sure you understand the question and have looked at all of the answer choices, since more than one may seem right at first.

Even if you're paying attention to the time, you may find yourself a little behind at some point. You should speed up to get back on track, but do so wisely. Don't panic; just take a few seconds less on each question until you're caught up. Don't guess without thinking, but do look through the answer choices and eliminate any you know are wrong. If you can get down to two choices, it is often worthwhile to guess from those. Once you've chosen an answer, move on and don't dwell on any that you skipped or had to hurry through. If a question was taking too long, chances are it was one of the harder ones, so you weren't as likely to get it right anyway.

On the other hand, if you find yourself getting ahead of schedule, it may be beneficial to slow down a little. The more quickly you work, the more likely you are to make a careless mistake that will affect your score. You've budgeted time for each question, so don't be afraid to spend that time. Practice an efficient but careful pace to get the most out of the time you have.

Secret Key #5 – Have a Plan for Guessing

When you're taking the test, you may find yourself stuck on a question. Some of the answer choices seem better than others, but you don't see the one answer choice that is obviously correct. What do you do?

The scenario described above is very common, yet most test takers have not effectively prepared for it. Developing and practicing a plan for guessing may be one of the single most effective uses of your time as you get ready for the exam.

In developing your plan for guessing, there are three questions to address:

- When should you start the guessing process?
- How should you narrow down the choices?
- Which answer should you choose?

When to Start the Guessing Process

Unless your plan for guessing is to select C every time (which, despite its merits, is not what we recommend), you need to leave yourself enough time to apply your answer elimination strategies. Since you have a limited amount of time for each question, that means that if you're going to give yourself the best shot at guessing correctly, you have to decide quickly whether or not you will guess.

Of course, the best-case scenario is that you don't have to guess at all, so first, see if you can answer the question based on your knowledge of the subject and basic reasoning skills. Focus on the key words in the question and try to jog your memory of related topics. Give yourself a chance to bring the knowledge to mind, but once you realize that you don't have (or you can't access) the knowledge you need to answer the question, it's time to start the guessing process.

It's almost always better to start the guessing process too early than too late. It only takes a few seconds to remember something and answer the question from knowledge. Carefully eliminating wrong answer choices takes longer. Plus, going through the process of eliminating answer choices can actually help jog your memory.

Summary: Start the guessing process as soon as you decide that you can't answer the question based on your knowledge.

How to Narrow Down the Choices

The next chapter in this book (**Test-Taking Strategies**) includes a wide range of strategies for how to approach questions and how to look for answer choices to eliminate. You will definitely want to read those carefully, practice them, and figure out which ones work best for you. Here though, we're going to address a mindset rather than a particular strategy.

Your odds of guessing an answer correctly depend on how many options you are choosing from.

Number of options left	5	4	3	2	1
Odds of guessing correctly	20%	25%	33%	50%	100%

You can see from this chart just how valuable it is to be able to eliminate incorrect answers and make an educated guess, but there are two things that many test takers do that cause them to miss out on the benefits of guessing:

- Accidentally eliminating the correct answer
- Selecting an answer based on an impression

We'll look at the first one here, and the second one in the next section.

To avoid accidentally eliminating the correct answer, we recommend a thought exercise called **the $5 challenge**. In this challenge, you only eliminate an answer choice from contention if you are willing to bet $5 on it being wrong. Why $5? Five dollars is a small but not insignificant amount of money. It's an amount you could afford to lose but wouldn't want to throw away. And while losing $5 once might not hurt too much, doing it twenty times will set you back $100. In the same way, each small decision you make—eliminating a choice here, guessing on a question there—won't by itself impact your score very much, but when you put them all together, they can make a big difference. By holding each answer choice elimination decision to a higher standard, you can reduce the risk of accidentally eliminating the correct answer.

The $5 challenge can also be applied in a positive sense: If you are willing to bet $5 that an answer choice *is* correct, go ahead and mark it as correct.

Summary: Only eliminate an answer choice if you are willing to bet $5 that it is wrong.

Which Answer to Choose

You're taking the test. You've run into a hard question and decided you'll have to guess. You've eliminated all the answer choices you're willing to bet $5 on. Now you have to pick an answer. Why do we even need to talk about this? Why can't you just pick whichever one you feel like when the time comes?

The answer to these questions is that if you don't come into the test with a plan, you'll rely on your impression to select an answer choice, and if you do that, you risk falling into a trap. The test writers know that everyone who takes their test will be guessing on some of the questions, so they intentionally write wrong answer choices to seem plausible. You still have to pick an answer though, and if the wrong answer choices are designed to look right, how can you ever be sure that you're not falling for their trap? The best solution we've found to this dilemma is to take the decision out of your hands entirely. Here is the process we recommend:

Once you've eliminated any choices that you are confident (willing to bet $5) are wrong, select the first remaining choice as your answer.

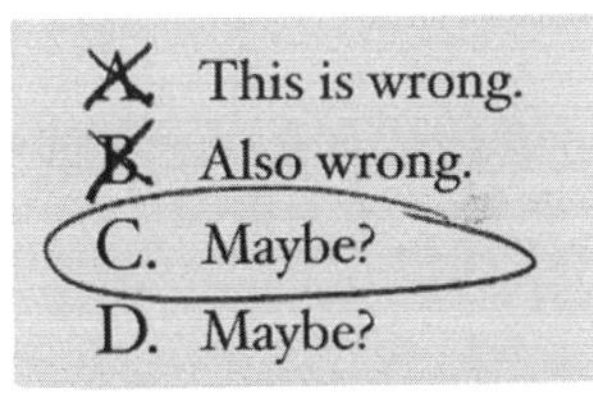

Whether you choose to select the first remaining choice, the second, or the last, the important thing is that you use some preselected standard. Using this approach guarantees that you will not be enticed into selecting an answer choice that looks right, because you are not basing your decision on how the answer choices look.

This is not meant to make you question your knowledge. Instead, it is to help you recognize the difference between your knowledge and your impressions. There's a huge difference between thinking an answer is right because of what you know, and thinking an answer is right because it looks or sounds like it should be right.

Summary: To ensure that your selection is appropriately random, make a predetermined selection from among all answer choices you have not eliminated.

Test-Taking Strategies

This section contains a list of test-taking strategies that you may find helpful as you work through the test. By taking what you know and applying logical thought, you can maximize your chances of answering any question correctly!

It is very important to realize that every question is different and every person is different: no single strategy will work on every question, and no single strategy will work for every person. That's why we've included all of them here, so you can try them out and determine which ones work best for different types of questions and which ones work best for you.

Question Strategies

✓ Read Carefully

Read the question and the answer choices carefully. Don't miss the question because you misread the terms. You have plenty of time to read each question thoroughly and make sure you understand what is being asked. Yet a happy medium must be attained, so don't waste too much time. You must read carefully and efficiently.

✓ Contextual Clues

Look for contextual clues. If the question includes a word you are not familiar with, look at the immediate context for some indication of what the word might mean. Contextual clues can often give you all the information you need to decipher the meaning of an unfamiliar word. Even if you can't determine the meaning, you may be able to narrow down the possibilities enough to make a solid guess at the answer to the question.

✓ Prefixes

If you're having trouble with a word in the question or answer choices, try dissecting it. Take advantage of every clue that the word might include. Prefixes can be a huge help. Usually, they allow you to determine a basic meaning. *Pre-* means before, *post-* means after, *pro-* is positive, *de-* is negative. From prefixes, you can get an idea of the general meaning of the word and try to put it into context.

✓ Hedge Words

Watch out for critical hedge words, such as *likely, may, can, often, almost, mostly, usually, generally, rarely,* and *sometimes.* Question writers insert these hedge phrases to cover every possibility. Often an answer choice will be wrong simply because it leaves no room for exception. Be on guard for answer choices that have definitive words such as *exactly* and *always.*

✓ Switchback Words

Stay alert for *switchbacks.* These are the words and phrases frequently used to alert you to shifts in thought. The most common switchback words are *but, although,* and *however.* Others include *nevertheless, on the other hand, even though, while, in spite of, despite,* and *regardless of.* Switchback words are important to catch because they can change the direction of the question or an answer choice.

☑ FACE VALUE

When in doubt, use common sense. Accept the situation in the problem at face value. Don't read too much into it. These problems will not require you to make wild assumptions. If you have to go beyond creativity and warp time or space in order to have an answer choice fit the question, then you should move on and consider the other answer choices. These are normal problems rooted in reality. The applicable relationship or explanation may not be readily apparent, but it is there for you to figure out. Use your common sense to interpret anything that isn't clear.

Answer Choice Strategies

☑ ANSWER SELECTION

The most thorough way to pick an answer choice is to identify and eliminate wrong answers until only one is left, then confirm it is the correct answer. Sometimes an answer choice may immediately seem right, but be careful. The test writers will usually put more than one reasonable answer choice on each question, so take a second to read all of them and make sure that the other choices are not equally obvious. As long as you have time left, it is better to read every answer choice than to pick the first one that looks right without checking the others.

☑ ANSWER CHOICE FAMILIES

An answer choice family consists of two (in rare cases, three) answer choices that are very similar in construction and cannot all be true at the same time. If you see two answer choices that are direct opposites or parallels, one of them is usually the correct answer. For instance, if one answer choice says that quantity *x* increases and another either says that quantity *x* decreases (opposite) or says that quantity *y* increases (parallel), then those answer choices would fall into the same family. An answer choice that doesn't match the construction of the answer choice family is more likely to be incorrect. Most questions will not have answer choice families, but when they do appear, you should be prepared to recognize them.

☑ ELIMINATE ANSWERS

Eliminate answer choices as soon as you realize they are wrong, but make sure you consider all possibilities. If you are eliminating answer choices and realize that the last one you are left with is also wrong, don't panic. Start over and consider each choice again. There may be something you missed the first time that you will realize on the second pass.

☑ AVOID FACT TRAPS

Don't be distracted by an answer choice that is factually true but doesn't answer the question. You are looking for the choice that answers the question. Stay focused on what the question is asking for so you don't accidentally pick an answer that is true but incorrect. Always go back to the question and make sure the answer choice you've selected actually answers the question and is not merely a true statement.

☑ EXTREME STATEMENTS

In general, you should avoid answers that put forth extreme actions as standard practice or proclaim controversial ideas as established fact. An answer choice that states the "process should be used in certain situations, if..." is much more likely to be correct than one that states the "process should be discontinued completely." The first is a calm rational statement and doesn't even make a definitive, uncompromising stance, using a hedge word *if* to provide wiggle room, whereas the second choice is far more extreme.

☑ Benchmark

As you read through the answer choices and you come across one that seems to answer the question well, mentally select that answer choice. This is not your final answer, but it's the one that will help you evaluate the other answer choices. The one that you selected is your benchmark or standard for judging each of the other answer choices. Every other answer choice must be compared to your benchmark. That choice is correct until proven otherwise by another answer choice beating it. If you find a better answer, then that one becomes your new benchmark. Once you've decided that no other choice answers the question as well as your benchmark, you have your final answer.

☑ Predict the Answer

Before you even start looking at the answer choices, it is often best to try to predict the answer. When you come up with the answer on your own, it is easier to avoid distractions and traps because you will know exactly what to look for. The right answer choice is unlikely to be word-for-word what you came up with, but it should be a close match. Even if you are confident that you have the right answer, you should still take the time to read each option before moving on.

General Strategies

☑ Tough Questions

If you are stumped on a problem or it appears too hard or too difficult, don't waste time. Move on! Remember though, if you can quickly check for obviously incorrect answer choices, your chances of guessing correctly are greatly improved. Before you completely give up, at least try to knock out a couple of possible answers. Eliminate what you can and then guess at the remaining answer choices before moving on.

☑ Check Your Work

Since you will probably not know every term listed and the answer to every question, it is important that you get credit for the ones that you do know. Don't miss any questions through careless mistakes. If at all possible, try to take a second to look back over your answer selection and make sure you've selected the correct answer choice and haven't made a costly careless mistake (such as marking an answer choice that you didn't mean to mark). This quick double check should more than pay for itself in caught mistakes for the time it costs.

☑ Pace Yourself

It's easy to be overwhelmed when you're looking at a page full of questions; your mind is confused and full of random thoughts, and the clock is ticking down faster than you would like. Calm down and maintain the pace that you have set for yourself. Especially as you get down to the last few minutes of the test, don't let the small numbers on the clock make you panic. As long as you are on track by monitoring your pace, you are guaranteed to have time for each question.

☑ Don't Rush

It is very easy to make errors when you are in a hurry. Maintaining a fast pace in answering questions is pointless if it makes you miss questions that you would have gotten right otherwise. Test writers like to include distracting information and wrong answers that seem right. Taking a little extra time to avoid careless mistakes can make all the difference in your test score. Find a pace that allows you to be confident in the answers that you select.

⊘ KEEP MOVING

Panicking will not help you pass the test, so do your best to stay calm and keep moving. Taking deep breaths and going through the answer elimination steps you practiced can help to break through a stress barrier and keep your pace.

Final Notes

The combination of a solid foundation of content knowledge and the confidence that comes from practicing your plan for applying that knowledge is the key to maximizing your performance on test day. As your foundation of content knowledge is built up and strengthened, you'll find that the strategies included in this chapter become more and more effective in helping you quickly sift through the distractions and traps of the test to isolate the correct answer.

Now that you're preparing to move forward into the test content chapters of this book, be sure to keep your goal in mind. As you read, think about how you will be able to apply this information on the test. If you've already seen sample questions for the test and you have an idea of the question format and style, try to come up with questions of your own that you can answer based on what you're reading. This will give you valuable practice applying your knowledge in the same ways you can expect to on test day.

Good luck and good studying!

Developing and Validating a Plan of Supply

Purpose

The purpose of sales and operations planning is the ongoing development of a practical plan encompassing all areas of the company in support of the overall business plan. Sales and operations planning are performed on the product family level and are used as the basis for the day-to-day product level manufacturing planning. The three primary inputs to the sales and operations planning process are the business plan, the anticipated demand, and the available resources. This information is used to develop and maintain a sales plan, indicating the planned volume of future sales per time period, and the production plan, the planned volume of future production per time period to support the sales plan. Sales and operations planning address two fundamental issues – the balance of supply and demand and the appropriate volume and mix for production.

Owner Responsibility

The owner of the sales and operations planning process is the person or group responsible for the wellbeing of the entire company if planning is universal, or the division to which the process applies if it is divided. Typically this responsibility falls to senior management as a group, and ultimately to the company president or chief executive officer (CEO), depending on the company's size. It is this process owner's responsibility to ensure that senior management supports the sales and operations planning process. A typical rule in a successful company is that no sales and operations planning representatives can miss or send a replacement to the monthly meetings. Attendance is required, and other activities and responsibilities must be scheduled accordingly. The ongoing, usually monthly, sales and operations planning meeting is the most important meeting in the company since it is when the company direction is determined.

Five Steps

The five steps of sales and operations planning are creating month-end reports, planning demand, planning supply, conducting a pre-sales and operations planning meeting, and conducting the sales and operations planning meeting. The month-end report is generated by the information technology department and serves as input in demand planning. Sales, marketing, customer service, and supply chain management personnel work together to plan actual and anticipated demand. Sales, marketing, manufacturing, materials, supply chain management, and master scheduling personnel work together to plan supply of purchased and manufactured parts to match the anticipated demand. In the pre-sales and operations planning meeting, personnel from sales, marketing, manufacturing, finance, materials management, planning, supply chain management, and master scheduling work together to propose a final solution or potential solutions for manufacturing to meet the demand, which is then decided upon in the executive sales and operations planning meeting.

Business Plan

The company business plan, any contingency planning factors, historical data, other forecast data, and the month-end reports are the inputs to the demand planning process. The business plan is the foundation of all other planning, including sales and operations planning in general and demand planning in particular. Contingency planning factors come into play when the material supply is unreliable and thus must be backed up, the forecasting is unreliable and thus requires additional buffer, or greater safety stock is needed for other reasons. The historical data, indicating the demand history, is key in predicting future demand along with other forecast data such as market trends, anticipated company changes, and so on. Finally, the month-end report indicates the progress on current sales and operations planning, and any necessary changes to the sales and marketing forecast can be finalized.

Sales and Marketing Forecast

The sales and marketing forecast, a current record of available resources, bills of resources, proposed sales plan, and previous production plan are all inputs to the supply planning process. The current record of available resources and the bills of resources, lists of resources needed to produce individual products, are used to balance available supply with the sales and marketing forecast, also known as the sales plan. Aggregate planning is performed to determine how best to meet the sales plan through production over the long term and resource planning is performed to reconcile the available resources with the sales and production plans. Changes can be made to both of these plans if deemed necessary.

Demand Planning

Integrated into the sales and operations planning process is the balancing of supply and demand, or resource and demand planning. If the available resources and the anticipated demand do not line up, they can be brought into balance through adjusting either the resources available or changing the anticipated demand to be filled.

The production plan, one primary output of sales and operations planning, specifies the production output by product family per time period. This is actually a statement of future goods available for sale and shipping. In combination with available inventory, the production plan provides the information necessary to develop a shipping schedule by product family. In the case of seasonal businesses, the production and shipping schedules may not correlate since goods produced are held in storage until peak sales times.

The production plan also provides the necessary production rate needed in manufacturing to maintain the plan. From the required production rate, the labor requirements can be calculated and planned per time period.

Pre-Sales and Operations Planning

The primary inputs to the pre-sales and operations planning meeting are the proposed sales and production plans from the supply planning phase, the proposals for changes to the sales and production plans from the supply planning phase, the current performance measurements, and the current inventory levels. Typical items to be considered in the pre-sales and operations planning meeting include orders currently on hand, current inventory levels, comparison of actual sales to planned sales for the previous month, comparison of actual production to planned production for the previous month, comparison of actual service level to the target service level for the previous month, and new product launches. The output of this meeting is proposed sales and production plans and recommended changes to resources and policies, all with appropriate supporting documentation to be considered and decided upon in the executive sales and operations planning meeting.

Executive Sales and Operations Planning

The inputs to the executive sales and operations planning meeting are the outputs from the pre-sales and operations planning meeting: the proposed sales and production plans and recommended changes to resources and policies. The executives must approve and commit to the approved changes and plans, verifying that they support the company objectives and strategic plan. The sales plan will drive sales and marketing, while the production plan drives materials planning and manufacturing. Changes to resources include action dates and identification of responsibilities.

Approval and commitment from the company executives provide integrated and effective execution of the plans.

Plan Evaluation

As the production plan is evaluated in the sales and operations planning meeting, there are three possible conclusions. The plan either fits well with the available resources, the plan underutilizes the available resources, or the plan exceeds the available resources. If the plan fits well with the available resources, it is accepted and executed. If the plan underutilizes available resources, management must decide if the underutilization is short-term or long-term. Short-term underutilization is not necessarily a problem. If the underutilization is long-term, management must decide how to handle it. Extra personnel can be laid off, but this is bad for morale and may not be cost effective if the laid-off personnel would eventually be replaced. Some companies use times like these for extensive employee training. If the plan over utilizes the available resources, management must decide to either change the plan or increase the resources. The resources can be increased on a short-term or long-term basis, whichever is appropriate.

Sales and Operations Planning Report

Through sales and operations planning, the sales and production plans to support the overall business strategy are developed. The sales and operations planning report is a comparison of the output sales plan and production plan with the purpose of discovering the net result of the combined plans on the company's inventory. This report is an application of the input/output control concept at the master planning level, to plan overall resources and corresponding output. The sales and/or production plans may be altered based on the report results. This technique is applicable in make-to-stock, make-to-order, engineer-to-order and assemble-to-order environments with appropriate adjustments.

In actual sales and operations planning reports in make-to-order, assemble-to-order, and engineer-to-order production environments, the planned sales, actual sales, planned production, actual production, planned backlog, actual backlog, and any resulting discrepancies and cumulative discrepancies are tracked for the past, present, and future. Adjustments in the future plan can then be made based on past history and current backlog. For example, if there have been discrepancies between forecast and actual sales and/or forecast and actual production resulting in actual backlog deficits or surpluses in comparison to the planned backlog, then adjustments to future production and/or sales can be made accordingly. The report is a tool used in ongoing sales and operations planning to keep the sales and production plans current and effective.

Backlog Changes

Backlog levels are of concern in make-to-order production environments, since that is where backlog is necessary. The primary reason for backlog level changes is the reduction of lead time experienced by customers. In order to reduce the lead time experienced by customers, the backlog level must be also reduced. Reducing the backlog level requires that the existing backlog be produced more quickly until the desired level is reached, at which point production can slow to the normal rate. Temporarily increasing the rate of production requires changing the master production schedule (MPS).

Inventory Changes

Inventory levels are of concern in make-to-stock production environments. There are three potential causes for inventory level changes. These potential causes are changes in forecast demand, frequency of delivery of supplies, and required service level. If the forecast demand changes, the master production schedule (MPS) quantities may change accordingly. MPS changes cause changes in material requirements, which may cause timing issues. A suitable planning time fence prevents problems of this nature. When the supply delivery frequency changes, the quantity to be delivered to meet manufacturing requirements may also change. If deliveries are made more often, a lower delivery quantity is required; if deliveries are made less often, a higher delivery quantity is required. When the required customer service level changes due to a change in company policy, the safety stock required to meet the customer service level changes accordingly. Changing the safety stock held will likely only affect the current manufacturing period by increasing or reducing the production quantity required. The MPS and material plan will change accordingly.

Sales and Production Plans

Both the sales plan and the production plan are developed in top management planning of the manufacturing planning and control system. Through sales and operation planning, the sales plan is developed from the business plan, the available and/or feasibly added manufacturing and financial resources, and the sales and marketing forecast demand for goods. The sales plan specifies, with full management agreement, the products anticipated to be sold by family per period. The production plan is developed to specify the products to be manufactured by family per quarter and per month in order to meet the sales plan. The monthly breakdown of the production plan is used by the master scheduler to develop a master schedule for manufacturing, and the quarterly breakdown is used to pinpoint future resources required for manufacturing.

Elements of Operations Management Planning

Master production scheduling – The operations management planning function of developing a detailed production plan, also known as an anticipated build schedule, from the more general production plan; the master production schedule (MPS) serves as the basis for all other manufacturing plans and schedules.

Rough-cut capacity planning – A tool used in operations management planning to verify the feasibility of the MPS by comparing it to the available manufacturing capacity.

Distribution planning – The operations management planning function of managing the dispersion of finished goods through controlling finished goods inventory supply and replenishment.

Material requirements planning (MRP) – The operations management planning function of determining a detailed material plan derived from the detailed material requirements, for both purchasing and internal manufacturing, to meet the master production schedule

Capacity requirements planning (CRP) – A tool used in operations management planning to break down the material plan into the individual operations required and compare them to the availability of the work centers involved

Planning data – All of the information that is used to support operations management planning including item master files, bills of material, and routing files

Elements of Operations Management Execution

Procurement – The operations management execution function of acquiring the materials necessary for production in a timely manner through order schedules and releases.

Production activity control (PAC) – The operations management execution function of controlling the volume of material in production through input-output control and establishing manufacturing priorities through dispatching.

Kanban control – The operations management execution function of replacing manufacturing materials as they are used; kanban control can be used in tandem with or in place of PAC.

Dispatching – The operations management execution function of communicating the current priority plan to manufacturing, most commonly through a daily dispatch list.

Input/output control – The operations management execution function of controlling production capacity in which both the planned and actual manufacturing inputs and outputs of individual work centers are monitored and compared and used to control the volume of work released into manufacturing.

Manufacturing Planning and Control Systems

A manufacturing planning and control system consists of three levels. The first level is top management planning, the second level is operations management planning, and the bottom level is operations management execution. Top management planning, which entails business planning and sales and operations planning, feeds into operations management planning. Operations management planning, including master production scheduling and materials requirements planning, feeds into operations management execution. Operations management execution encompasses procurement, kanban control, and production activity control. Additional elements of manufacturing planning and control are resource requirements planning, associated with sales and operations planning; rough-cut capacity planning, associated with master production scheduling; capacity requirements planning, associated with material requirements planning; and distribution planning and planning data within operations management planning.

Elements of Top Management Planning

Business planning – The top management planning function in which an overall future plan for the organization is created, including organizational direction and anticipated business volume.

Sales and operations planning – The top management planning function of developing overall sales and production plans based on the business plan, manufacturing resources and financial resources; the approved sales and production plans are a commitment to manufacturing and an authorization to proceed.

Resource requirements planning – A tool used in top management planning to verify the feasibility of the sales and production plans developed in sales and operations planning by comparing it to the available resources.

Schedule of Manufacturing

The production plan is the schedule for manufacturing. The schedule extends as far into the future as the lead time for adding resources to the manufacturing process. Once the initial production plan is developed, it is simply revised and extended at the monthly sales and operations planning meetings. Quarterly, an additional quarter of planning is added to the end of the schedule, and the first quarter on the schedule is broken down into monthly plans. On a monthly basis, another month's plan is given to the master scheduler to add to the master production plan (MPS), the previous month's performance is reviewed, sales provides updated forecasting, and manufacturing identifies potential problems with the next month's schedule. This information is used to revise the month's plan as necessary, with management agreement and commitment.

Production Rate

The production rate is the is the number of production units, cases, or some other measure to be manufactured per hour, shift, day, week, or other time period in order to meet the requirements in the time frame required. Determining the production rate is a necessary step in effective management of manufacturing. The production plan must meet the required production rate, and is expressed aggregately, or in family groups. Manufacturing families are groups of items produced with the same resources, and do not necessarily line up with the sales families. Once the aggregate production plan is proposed, resource requirements planning are performed to verify that the necessary resources are available to execute the plan and the plan is accepted or adjusted as necessary. Items that are not manufactured internally but are purchased and resold are also accounted for in some way in the master schedule.

Sales Plan

Once the sales and production plans are agreed upon and committed to in the sales and operations planning meeting, the sales plan is distributed to the sales department and the production plan is distributed to the master scheduler. The sales department breaks the sales plan down into individual end items and targets for regions, areas, and individual representatives. The master scheduler breaks the monthly production plan quantities into daily or weekly quantities and the family groups into end items for the master production schedule (MPS). The MPS is then used as the basis for material resource planning (MRP) to establish specific schedules for ordering and manufacturing goods at all levels.

Trade Offs

During the sales and operations planning process, there are many trade-offs made. Any decision has an impact on the process as a whole and its interrelationships. Management must balance objectives with the costs incurred to meet those objectives. For example, higher customer service levels require higher inventory levels, which incur greater inventory costs. In general, it is desirable to maximize the customer service level and minimize inventory costs. Management must make some trade-off between the two to reach a workable target. Maintaining low inventory levels, which is desirable, requires smaller, more frequent manufacturing runs, which are less efficient. Once again, some trade-off must be made between minimizing inventory and maximizing manufacturing efficiency. In situations where manufacturing capacity is limited or at a premium, lower efficiency is not an option. The factors are all interrelated and trade-offs appropriate for the given situation must be made.

In service environments, the production plan developed in sales and operations planning specifies the individual contracts or contract families over time in hours or dollars. The master scheduler plans the customer orders based on the personnel and support required to complete the job. In a distribution environment, products are either manufactured or purchased and then distributed to customers. A distribution company may handle products from multiple manufacturers. The production, or in this case distribution, plan developed in sales and operations planning would specify sales per time period by product family, and perhaps additionally per geographic region. Stock is controlled through a replenishment system or distribution requirements planning (DRP) in order to meet the plan.

Resource Planning

Through resource requirements planning, which also called resource planning, long-term resource requirements are anticipated, the future resource load by key resource category is determined, future requirements are balanced across the available capacity, and feasibility of meeting the required performance measurements is verified. This is done per production family using the production plan and the bills of resources for each family group. In short, the plan is examined and compared to available capacity, the loading is balanced across the available capacity if possible, and the plan and/or the resources are adjusted if necessary. It is simply the process of verifying the feasibility of the production plan with respect to available resources and making any necessary adjustments to avoid resource availability problems in the future. In addition to the production plan and the bills of resources, historical performance data is used.

Bill of Resources

A bill of resource, which is also called a load profile, is a record of all resources required to build one production unit. Resources at all levels of production are included, but only the key primary resources are typically listed. Resource requirements planning calculations are performed by multiplying the product quantity per time period specified in the production plan by the resources necessary per item specified in the bill of resources. This calculation is performed for each family group, and then the overall resource requirements are added together to determine the total resource requirements per time period. These totals are then compared to the available resources per time period specified in the work center or resource files.

Make-to-Stock Production

In an actual sales and operations planning report in a make-to-stock production environment, the planned sales, actual sales, planned production, actual production, planned inventory, actual inventory, and any resulting discrepancies and cumulative discrepancies are tracked for the past, present, and future. Adjustments in the future plan can then be made based on past history and current inventory. For example, if there have been discrepancies between forecast and actual sales and/or forecast and actual production resulting in actual inventory deficits or surpluses in comparison to the planned inventory, then adjustments to future production and/or sales can be made accordingly. The report is a tool used in ongoing sales and operations planning to keep the sales and production plans current and effective.

In a make-to-order production environment, the logic used to determine the production plan when a level scheduling strategy is used is forecast sales plus the starting backlog minus the required ending backlog is the production plan, with the production spread evenly over the time periods. The backlog is the total of unfilled customer orders held by the company. The backlog acts as a buffer in situations when sales or production vary from the plan, ensuring that there is always work in process so that the scheduling remains level. This logic also applies to engineer-to-order and assemble-to-order environments.

Balanced Production Plan

In creating a balanced production plan, there are three practical considerations that must be made: the production volume necessary to meet the proposed sales plan, the availability of resources and capacity to meet the proposed sales plan, and the demand pattern of the proposed sales plan. The demand pattern can be constant, seasonal, or somewhere in between. To deal with seasonal demand patterns, there are many possible strategies, including providing the resources to meet the demand period by period, which leaves the problem of what to do with those resources in non-peak periods, and increasing the available resources in steps, which is particularly applicable in growing markets.

Chase Scheduling

When a chase scheduling production strategy is used, the production per period is equal to the projected sales for that period. The production volume varies with the forecast sales volume, and the inventory holds steady. The difficulty inherent in chase scheduling is that the labor and resources must be available to meet production requirements in peak periods, even though the same quantity of labor and resources is not necessary in other periods. A variable work force or the ability to move laborers around between product lines as necessary is required. Chase scheduling is usually not feasible unless there are flexible compensating products to take up the slack in resources and manpower.

Combination or Hybrid Strategy

With a combination or hybrid production strategy, the production rate is held steady at a higher rate than is usually necessary, with additional production added in peak time periods. The inventory level changes since the production rate and shipment rates vary. In most periods, the production rate is higher than the shipment rate increasing the inventory, and in peak periods both inventory and extra production meet the higher demand. The inventory acts as a buffer, but to a lesser degree than in chase scheduling. This strategy is also more stable than chase scheduling. The challenge with this strategy is how to meet the additional production added in peak time periods. The extra capacity can be provided through subcontracting, adding a second shift, or reassigning workers from other product lines.

Volume and Variety

The variety and volume of goods produced determine the manufacturing environment needed. A company should first determine the volume and variety of products necessary to reach their strategic goals, and then establish a manufacturing environment accordingly. Volume refers to the number of items produced, while variety refers to the number of types of items produced. There is an inverse relationship between the two. Factories usually make large amounts of a few set products, or small amounts of many specialized products. The four types of manufacturing environments are job shop (high variety, low volume), batch manufacture (somewhat high variety, somewhat low volume), line manufacture (somewhat low variety, somewhat high volume), and continuous manufacture (low variety, high volume).

Job Shop

A job shop is the lowest volume, highest variety manufacturing environment in which a wide range of general equipment is organized according to function and staffed by skilled personnel who can follow specifications for specialized products. Goods go through production according to a specified routing, which is different for each item produced. Goods are produced according to the individual customer's requirements, and small numbers of a wide variety of items are manufactured. Quality and timeliness are key, while price is secondary. Job shops are typically employed in make-to-order production environments.

Batch Manufacturing

Batch manufacturing is a somewhat low volume, high variety manufacturing facility similar to a job shop, but on a larger scale with less specialization, so there is less variety and greater volume produced. Batches of goods are produced to fill a wide range of orders, but orders are repetitive, or even standard. Since there is repetition, standing routings and manufacturing instructions as well as tooling and fixtures are provided. Capacity requirements planning (CRP) is employed. Batch manufacturing is typically utilized in make-to-stock production environments with demand forecasts. Price is a more important competitive consideration than in a job shop.

Line Manufacturing

Line manufacturing is a somewhat high volume, low variety manufacturing environment in which specialized equipment is used to produce a limited range of similar, standardized goods in somewhat high volumes. All of the goods produced proceed through the same line or sequence of manufacturing operations. Mixed-model and rate-based scheduling, master production scheduling (MPS), and material requirements planning (MRP) are used. Price is the most common order-winning strategy, and the production environment is typically make-to-stock with forecast requirements. Line manufacturing can also be used in assemble-to-order environments, with an additional final assembly schedule customizing products to customer orders.

Continuous Manufacturing

Continuous manufacturing is the highest volume, lowest variety manufacturing environment similar to line manufacturing but with even more specialized equipment and less variety of goods produced. It is a manufacturing environment in which highly specialized equipment is used to produce one or a very few type(s) of set goods in high volumes at an extremely low cost. Product changes and new products occur rarely. Manufacturing occurs twenty-four hours per day, seven days per week. In continuous manufacturing, price is typically the order-winning strategy, and the production environment is make-to-stock with forecast requirements for the standard product(s) produced.

Financial Considerations

High-volume and low-variety manufacturing are usually paired. High-volume, low-variety manufacturing is generally the least expensive production method for a given product, and is thus employed when a company has chosen price as their order-winning strategy. These factories typically produce only one product, or a handful of similar products.

Low-volume and high-variety manufacturing are also usually paired. Low-volume, high- variety manufacturing is typically employed when a company has chosen customization or quality as their order-winning strategy. Within this manufacturing environment, inventory investment and other associated costs are high because of the large number of raw materials and components required. Part commonality, the purposeful use of parts already stocked when designing new products or processes, is a strategy for minimizing these costs.

Product Life Cycle

A product's position in its life cycle significantly affects the type of manufacturing environment necessary to meet the demand for the product. In general, low manufacturing volume is sufficient in the early stages of the life cycle, followed by increased volume as the market responds to the new product, and ending with low volume as the product's life closes. The six life-cycle stages are pre-product development, product development, testing and introduction, rapid growth, steady state, and phasing out. It may be necessary to have different manufacturing methods at different stages. Demand forecasting must be used for each stage. Even after the product's life cycle ends support and spare parts must be available for those still in use in the field.

Production Planning Terms

Month-end report – A summary and review of previous performance created to inform the future planning process, with emphasis placed on comparing actual sales, production, inventory, and customer service level performance to the planned targets.

Statistical forecast – A theoretical future forecast created by information technology personnel based on analysis of historical data and relevant company policies to be used in the demand planning process.

Field sales worksheet – A record of sales activity logged by individual sales personnel recording companies visited, the outcomes of the visits, customer problems, and anticipated future sales, to be used in planning future demand and improving customer service.

Management forecast – Qualitative forecasts developed by management after consideration all of all known factors affecting sales.

Capacity constraint – A limitation of available capacity that restricts manufacturing

Constraints management – A manufacturing management philosophy based on the Theory of Constraints utilizing techniques such as drum-buffer-rope scheduling and buffer management to overcome constraints.

Project Assessment

Project Proposals

One role of upper management in sales and operations planning is the assessment of proposed projects to be undertaken by the company. Project proposals include a description of the project, an analysis of the financial and non-financial benefits to be reaped from the project, the costs and cost timelines associated with the project, the investment recovery time, and the basis on which these predictions have been made. Management must review these proposals to determine if the proposed projects would provide competitive advantage, support the company's strategic plan and order-winning strategy, and fit in with the company's current financial situation and environment. Management must also consider issues of interdependency between projects.

Non-Financial Costs

Some non-financial costs associated with undertaking or rejecting new projects can be increased workload on personnel, loss of competitive advantage and market position, and effective support of the company strategy, order qualifiers, and order winners. Projects may have a low financial cost but a significant impact on workload. Workload and resulting productivity costs must be considered carefully, especially if staff is already overloaded. The current market environment and a company's market position are also important considerations. If a company is the clear industry leader, improvement projects may provide too little advantage for the cost. Conversely, if a new technology or methodology is overtaking the market, the result of not embracing it can be loss of competitive advantage and market position. Supporting the up-to-date company strategy, order qualifiers, and order winners is essential to successful business. New projects can promote or hinder that support. Obviously, hindering that support is too high a price. Conversely, not implementing a good plan for that support may also carry too high a price.

Financial Implications

In sales and operations planning, not only are sales and production plans developed, but these plans are also evaluated for their financial implications. Using the sales and production plans, which specify product family volume per time period to be manufactured and sold, cash flow and profit can be forecast for the same time horizon. If the planned volumes are low, both product turnover and resulting income will be low. There is a minimum turnover threshold at which the plant can operate effectively. Conversely, when planned volumes are high, turnover and profit are also high, but the required capacity is high as well. If the capacity requirement exceeds availability, subcontracting can be utilized, and capacity can be increased in the long-term if necessary. Financial ratios such as return on investment and stock turns can also be used to evaluate the plans.

ROI

Return on investment – A technique for financial evaluation of production plans in which the relative return on an investment is calculated as the percentage of the initial investment amount produced; ROI = (income – costs)/investment; ROI can be increased by increasing the income generated, decreasing the associated costs, or decreasing the associated investment.

STOCK RETURNS

Stock turns – A technique for financial evaluation of production plans in which the annual cost of goods sold is divided by the average inventory held to determine the number of annual stock turns; stock turns are not a good foundation for comparisons between companies, but rather in comparing performance within a company over time

STAKEHOLDERS

A company's suppliers, management, employees, customers, and stockholders all hold a vested interest in the outcome of the sales and operations planning process. The plan must meet the needs of each of these groups. Suppliers want fulfillment and extension of existing agreements, management wants execution of the strategic plan, employees want job security, customers want a reliable supply of goods and customer support, and stockholders want an acceptable return on their investment. Management must consider all of these needs and do their best to plan sales and operations to meet these needs to retain good relationships with all groups if possible.

TIME HORIZON

When it comes to manpower, the timing horizon must be set such that there is sufficient time available for hiring and training the necessary workers for the job to be done. In highly specialized industries this can take up to a year, so these companies would need to know a year in advance that the workforce needs expansion. A company must set their sales and operations planning horizon far enough into the future to be able to acquire and train personnel in time to meet the increased manpower demand.

When it comes to facilities, it takes a considerable length of time to research, propose, and justify the expansion; to gain management approval for the project, especially in a multi-national business setting; and to actually construct the building(s). A two to three year sales and operations planning horizon is not unreasonable if sufficient time is to be available to execute the plans from the time that the need for the expansion is known.

The timing horizon required for equipment planning varies considerably with the industry and company environment. Standard equipment purchased off-the-shelf is quick and easy to obtain, but attaining specialized capital equipment is slow and expensive. Similar to facilities expansion, equipment acquisition for capacity expansion requires initial research, proposal, and justification and management approval, along with time for acquisition, installation, and fine-tuning. The planning horizon must be far enough into the future to allow the time necessary for all of this before the equipment demand is felt.

The current trend is for companies to use money within the company to pay for major projects. This is most commonly done through inventory reduction, which takes time if the customer service level is to be maintained. The sales and operations planning horizon must extend far enough into the future to allow the freeing up of internal financial resources to finance manpower, facilities, and/or equipment expansion before they are necessary.

PROJECT ASSESSMENT TERMS

Payback method – a financial evaluation technique for proposed projects in which the time required to recover the project investment is calculated; the payback is calculated by dividing the initial financial investment by the resulting annual net income to determine a payback period in years.

Average return on investment – a financial evaluation technique for proposed projects in which relative return for the investment is calculated as a percentage of the invested amount the net earnings produce; average return on investment is calculated by averaging the project's annual net return over its useful life and dividing by the initial investment.

Net present value method – a financial evaluation technique for proposed projects in which the future gain is converted to current dollars and compared to the investment required; net present value is calculated by multiplying the future earnings by an appropriate factor to make the conversion to current dollars.

Measuring Performance

There is no single solution or process which can be applied in order to measure all types of organizations. It is important to create a clear and consistent direction to measure performance. Without clear goals, it might be impossible to recognize whether the measurement is relevant. The criteria for measurement should be established by people who understand the whole picture of the company and can identify important key issues for consideration. For example, in order to measure quality - the evaluator should be the person involved closely with the organization or the department. The evaluator must identify the relationship between things to measure and its level of satisfaction which can be accepted as successful performance.

Needs for new measures include the following:

- Reevaluate existing measures - the change team will understand and be able to identify the mistakes and requirements which are useful for new measures.
- Measure the whole processes, not just the results. Result-oriented measures indicate problems, not the way to solve them.
- Measures should foster goal-driven teamwork. Shared-process measurements create an environment of goal-driven teamwork.
- Measures should be an integrated set derived from company strategy.
- Measures should have an external focus whenever possible; they should compare the performance with others in order to see the whole picture of the organization.

Customer Service Levels

Customer Identity

The first step in establishing the customer service level is defining the customer. The customer can be the end user of a product, another manufacturer who incorporates the item into their own product, or the next stage of internal manufacturing. After the customer is identified, what the customer wants, or at the very least what the customer will put up with, must be ascertained. As the customer service level increases, the cost of the customer service level increases exponentially. Management must determine a compromise between meeting customer desires and the associated cost. Once the desired customer service level is set, performance must be measured and improved.

Cost

Higher customer service levels produce more satisfied customers but require a higher inventory investment. As the customer service level increases, the cost of the customer service level increases exponentially. The primary cost associated with maintaining the customer service level is safety stock. In addition to the desired customer service level, the quantity of safety stock is dependent on demand variability and replenishment lead time. Through these interdependencies, management can see the relationship between cost and customer service level and determine a compromise between meeting customer desires and the associated cost.

Targeted Service Level

Management sets a target service level, and then the actual service level provided must be monitored and compared to that target. The customer service level provided is defined as the percentage of customer orders met from stock in a make-to-stock business or met from the production schedule in a make-to-order business by the customer's requested delivery date and in the customer requested quantities. There are two formulas for calculating the service level provided. Service level = (number of orders met/total number of orders)*100 or service level = (1 - (number of orders not met/total number of orders))*100.

Inventory Levels

Total Inventory Levels

A company's total inventory level is very important due to the high cost of maintaining it as well as the associated customer service level provided. It usually falls to the materials division or department to maintain the inventory within the predetermined target levels. If the inventory drops too low, then the customer service level drops below its target, and if the inventory gets too high, then costs increase and profits decrease. Methods of inventory measurement and reporting include absolute value of the inventory, day's coverage, and the number of inventory turns.

MRP

Material resource planning is typically used to determine what raw materials and purchased parts are necessary for manufacturing, but MRP does not actually control inventory levels. Company policy must set order quantities and frequency. If MRP is not used, then a replenishment system such as the order point method must be in place. This system results in higher inventory levels since it is based on averages and assumes that stock must always be in place whether current planning calls for it or not. Like MRP, the order point replenishment system is affected by the order quantity and frequency set. In both cases, ABC scheduling of replenishment reduces the average inventory level.

WIP

The level of work in process (WIP) inventory is determined by the manufacturing lead time. The longer the lead time is, the greater the amount of work in process will be. The manufacturing lead time is heavily influenced by the ratio of load to available capacity, since the greater this ratio is the more work is released; and more work produces longer queues and lead times. Current manufacturing philosophy tends toward maintaining sufficient capacity to minimize lead times and reduce WIP inventory. Through the use of just in time (JIT) manufacturing methods such as work cells, overlapping, and queue and wait time reduction, lead times and WIP can be reduced even more.

Finished Goods

In make-to-stock production environments, the master schedule drives manufacturing to meet the production plan. The resulting finished goods inventory level should then correspond to the sales plan in order to meet the forecast sales. Customer orders are filled from the finished goods inventory. The actual level of finished goods inventory at a given time is also a function of the stock replenishment system used, manufacturing batch quantities, and frequency of receipt of materials into the warehouse to supply manufacturing. When the periodic review method of inventory replenishment is used, the target inventory level is a theoretical maximum that should never be reached, but rather ordered up to.

Inventory Terms

Absolute value of inventory – A means of inventory measurement and reporting in which the total of the standard values of all items held in stock is calculated.

Day's coverage – A means of inventory measurement and reporting in which the absolute value of the inventory is divided by the average daily demand value to determine the number of average days' stock held.

Inventory turns – A means of inventory measurement and reporting in which the annual cost of goods sold is divided by the average inventory held to determine the number of annual stock turns, an indication of how long inventory is held before it is sold.

Important Terms

Business plan – The long-term (covering five years or more) master or strategic plan set by senior management, usually yearly, and followed by a company in all of its other planning and decision-making; sales and operations planning is based on the business plan.

Aggregate demand planning – Planning based on demand that is forecast at the product family level nationally through the marketing function using qualitative methods, modeling, and/or current economic information and then reconciled to the local, product-level demand forecast developed by the sales force; sales and operations planning is based on aggregate demand planning.

Aggregate resource planning – Planning based on the overall future availability of resources, identified as individual resources available per time period with the same identification and units of measure used in the resource bills of material; sales and operations planning is based on aggregate resource planning.

Sales plan – The planned volume of sales per time period by product family agreed to by management, which drives the corresponding production plan; the sales plan is developed through sales and operations planning and is analogous to the production plan so that the two can be easily used together.

Production plan – The planned volume of production per time period by product family agreed to by management to support the sales plan and drive the master production schedule (MPS); the production plan is developed through sales and operations planning and is analogous to the sales plan so that the two can be easily used together.

Resource utilization – The effective use of resources, which differs from maximizing utilization of resources as has been done in the past; sale and operations planning involves evaluation of the plans developed for resource utilization.

Cumulative charting – A production planning tool in which the planned cumulative production and the planned cumulative shipments are graphed together to show the resulting inventory at any given stage of the plans.

Level scheduling – A production strategy in which manufacturing is maintained at a consistent rate regardless of current demand and surplus is held until needed in finished goods inventory; the disadvantage of level scheduling is holding inventory and associated costs.

Chase scheduling – A production strategy in which the manufacturing rate follows the shipment plan and thus the forecast product demand with safety stock as a buffer against forecast errors and other problems; the disadvantage of level scheduling is the variation in labor requirements for manufacturing and the uncertainty of meeting demand at peak times.

Combination scheduling – A production strategy in which level and chase scheduling are combined such that production is at a consistent rate but augmented in peak periods; combination scheduling is also referred to as hybrid scheduling.

Identifying, Quantifying and Assessing Demand

Company Strategies

Personnel

There are generally three groups of personnel involved in the strategic planning process. These three groups are outside or external stakeholders, top-level company management, and general management and specialized staff. The outside or external stakeholders are individuals or groups outside of the company who have a vested interest in the company's success, including the company's suppliers, customers, and stockholders, related unions, and the community at large. Top-level company management is comprised of the company's senior management team. General management and specialized staff include lower-level management such as departmental leaders and personnel with special expertise necessary in the planning process.

Developing a Corporate Strategy

The customers, the market environment, the legal limitations and requirements, social conventions, economic conditions, and technological issues are all factors to consider when developing a corporate strategy. The customer should be the primary focus. The market environment includes both competition and external influences on sales. Legal issues can include import controls, pollution regulations, and safety legislation. Social conventions can strongly affect the types of products purchased or rejected at a given place at a given time. The general economic situation profoundly impacts business success and technological issues impact how companies do business as well as what is expected in the marketplace. The rise of the internet and e-commerce is a significant technological issue in the current marketplace.

The three different approaches generally used for developing business strategies are price leadership, product differentiation, and customer focus.--In price leadership, the business strategy is based on low product prices. A range of products are manufactured through a reliable and respected process and sold for comparatively low prices.--In product differentiation, the business strategy is based on unique product characteristics that set the product(s) apart from the competing product(s).--In customer focus, the business strategy is based on meeting customer needs and providing a high level of customer service and responsiveness.

Keeping Strategies Current

The corporate strategy, including the business strategy, must be kept current since the considerations upon which it is based are changeable. Customers, market environment, legal regulations, social conventions, economic situation, and technological issues all change over time. The company's own self-assessment should also change over time. If the strategy does not change as well, then it becomes obsolete because of the failure to respond to change. Additionally, as the strategy remains unchanged, individuals within the company develop their own interpretations of the strategy to deal with changes and company unity is eroded and ultimately lost.

Manufacturing Strategies

There are many considerations involved in developing a manufacturing strategy. The manufacturing strategy is often overlooked, but can provide long-term competitive edge if handled well. Some of the manufacturing strategy considerations include the facilities, especially their location and price; capacity, especially technology and price; quality, both goals and inspections methods; information systems, and how they relate to competition; organization of staff, centralized or decentralized; integration, determining what functions to perform internally and what to delegate to suppliers; and processes and technologies, especially preventive maintenance to avoid breakdown and stoppage costs.

MPS

The master production schedule (MPS) is the primary ingredient of the manufacturing planning and control system. All elements within the system work together to produce and follow the MPS. The MPS is the plan for actual manufacturing, as well as the basis for material and capacity planning to support the manufacturing plan. Finally, the MPS is the guide for committing to orders for goods that are not yet complete by detailing what goods will be ready when. From this role, it is obvious that the MPS must be up-to-date. An accurate and current MPS, through continual updating as changes occur, is essential for proper functioning of the manufacturing and control system.

MRP

Material requirements planning (MRP) is the process by which the material supply is orchestrated to meet material demand. The basic principles of MRP are determination of what materials to order, when to order them, how much of them to order, and when to schedule them for delivery. Characteristics of MRP include addressing the nature of demand (independent vs. dependent), calculation of net requirements, maintenance of material and capacity priorities, reduction of shortages, and focus on the future rather than the past. Material orders are linked to future material requirements, with the goal of balancing supply and demand. MRP logic begins at the end, at the final products required on particular dates according to the master production schedule (MPS), and works backwards to establish what materials will be necessary on what dates to meet the MPS requirements.

PAC

Production activity control (PAC) must facilitate the detailed scheduling of the individual manufacturing operations throughout the production process including start and completion dates, the assignment through proper loading of work to the shops and/or workstations with appropriate documentation, current tracking of work in progress (WIP) throughout manufacturing for location and monitoring purposes, acceptance and recording of necessary production details as required by the manufacturer, a dispatching system for communicating current work and priority assignments to manufacturing, and the issuing of relevant reports as required. The PAC process in use must also be accessible for provision of good customer service, primarily through reliable information regarding completion dates for the commitment of goods to customers.

Production Environments

Make-to-stock – Production environments in which standard products are manufactured in response to the forecast demand for those products, stored in inventory, and sold as they are when customers order them.

Make-to-order – Production environments in which products are manufactured in response to actual customer orders, rather than in response to forecast demand; subcategories of make-to-order include design-to-order, engineer-to-order, assemble-to-order, and package-to-order.

Design-to-order – Make-to-order production environments in which the product is designed and then built in response to customer orders.

Engineer-to-order – make-to-order production environments in which finished products are engineered and produced from standard, on-hand assemblies in response to customer orders.

Assemble-to-order – Make-to-order production environments in which final products are produced from standard, on-hand major assemblies (i.e. final assembly) in response to customer orders.

Package-to-order – Make-to-order production environments in which finished products are held in storage without packaging and packaged in response to customer orders since specialized packaging is required.

FORECASTING DEMAND

A demand forecast is a prediction or estimation of the future orders for a product based on projected market need or desire for that product. These demand forecasts can be calculated through mathematical formulas based on historical information, estimated from informal sources, or determined through a combination of both of these methods. When making a demand forecast, it is important to determine the materials and/or products to be forecast, the level of detail required in the forecast, the pool of data to be drawn from to generate the forecast, and the immediate and future uses for the forecast.

When estimating future demand, it is better to work with product families than with individual products. Less work is necessary due to the common raw materials and parts often used. The forecast itself should not be a precise number, but rather a range of numbers defined either by a high and low, or an average with expected deviation. Forecasts are predictions only and as such are inaccurate. Inaccuracy must be expected and planned for. Furthermore, the greater the length of time for which the forecast is made, the greater the expected inaccuracy. Long-range forecasting should be used sparingly and only as necessary. Ultimate commitment of resources should occur as late as possible on as short a forecast as possible. Forecasting should not be used unless absolutely necessary and it is only necessary for items experiencing independent demand. Dependent demand should always be calculated. Demand forecasts and the actual demand should be tracked and compared with the purpose of improving forecast accuracy in the future.

Product demand should be forecast for distribution inventories, finished goods inventories, module inventory when planning bills are utilized and service parts inventory. It is important to forecast demand for distribution inventories by distribution site or depot, so that stock will be sufficient at each site to meet the demand at that site. It is important to forecast demand for finished goods inventories when products are sold from stock so that there will be sufficient product available for sale. It is important to forecast demand for assembly modules rather than finished goods when there are infinite possible end configurations for sale. These individualized end items cannot be predicted, but the demand for modules to construct them can. Demand for service parts for internal and external use must also be forecast and held in inventory for continued smooth operation of manufacturing as well as good customer service.

Demand forecasts are crucial to manufacturing because this information is used for all business planning, including inventory planning, capacity planning, lead time management, and date commitments to customers. In short, manufacturing uses the demand forecast to be prepared with products when they are thought to be necessary. Manufacturing capacity, inventory on hand, and available sell dates of finished goods are planned based on the predicted demand. In make-to-order production environments, demand forecasts are made for the assemblies and parts used in final assembly rather than on the finished goods themselves. The level of detail required in the forecasting is dependent on the actual use of the forecast. A greater level of detail is required for short-term planning than for long-term planning.

MAKE-TO-ORDER AND ENGINEER-TO-ORDER

Forecasting can be used in two different ways in make-to-order production environments. One forecasting method used is to develop a forecast to provide the necessary materials for production after an order has been received. This method involves longer lead times. The alternative is to use forecasts to stock necessary raw materials and components beforehand so that production can begin as soon as an order is received, shortening the lead time. In both cases, production does not begin until an order is received.

In engineer-to-order environments, forecasts can be made of standard components and major subassemblies, which are then used to configure the individually designed orders. Some specialized parts and supplies may not be forecast but acquired as needed in response to customer orders.

DEMAND FORECASTING TECHNIQUES

Expert judgment – A qualitative demand forecasting technique in which a group of individuals work together as a team to predict future demand; expert judgment should be used together with one of the intrinsic quantitative methods when possible

Management estimation – A qualitative demand forecasting technique in which management predictions are based on the instinct of the manager making the prediction; management estimation can be a good feasibility check for more quantitative forecasting methods

Historical analogy –A qualitative demand forecasting technique used in the case of new products in which historical demand for similar products is used to predict the demand patterns for the short-term until the product builds a sales history of its own

DEMAND PATTERNS

When using internal historical sales data, the data must be plotted over time for patterns to emerge. Historical patterns can then be used to predict future sales. Some typical demand patterns include level, trend, seasonal, cyclic, and irregular sales. A level demand pattern is steady because sales hold constant over time. A demand trend is a consistent increase (positive trend) or decrease (negative trend) in sales over time. In a seasonal demand pattern sales vary substantially by season, but the seasonal pattern repeats itself, as is often the case for season-specific goods. A cyclic demand pattern is one in which sales are inconsistent over a fairly short time period, but the inconsistency repeats itself, as is the case for products purchased around payday. An irregular demand pattern is completely inconsistent and cannot be predicted other than through a percentage of fluctuation. It is important to note that more than one or even all demand patterns can contribute elements to the demand for a particular product or product family.

INDEPENDENT AND DEPENDENT DEMANDS

Independent demand – Demand for material, usually finished goods, which cannot be calculated internally and is unrelated to internal factors, but which must be predicted; for example, a company's estimation or projection of the amount of finished goods that will be necessary to meet customer orders, based on past history or market indicators, in a given future time period is an independent demand on manufacturing.

Dependent demand – Demand for materials, usually raw materials or component parts, which is not predicted or forecast, but rather can be calculated from the independent demand; for example, once the independent demand for finished goods is forecast, the number of component parts and raw materials necessary to manufacture the forecast number of finished goods can be calculated; there is a clear relationship between independent and dependent demands, with dependent demand relying on independent demand.

Forecasting Terms

Aggregate forecast – An overall demand forecast made for a group of products, usually a product family or a brand; aggregate forecasts are usually more accurate than the corresponding sum of individual or disaggregate forecasts.

Disaggregate forecast – A demand forecast made for individual products within a product family, brand, or other group rather than for the product family, brand, or group as a whole.

Family forecast – An overall, aggregate, or group demand forecast made for a particular product family.

Individual forecast – A product forecast made for a particular product, separate from its product family, brand, or group.

Stable forecast – A fairly accurate or certain demand forecast based on a long history of consistent sales that are expected to continue in the time period of the forecast.

Unstable forecast – A demand forecast based solely on estimations, and not on historical data, as is usually the case with new products.

Data

Mathematical methods for forecasting product demand based on past history can require from two to five years worth of information, so long-term recording and storage of demand, sales, and shipment data is essential to the forecasting process. The end user of the data usually has little or no control over the data recorders, especially if data is being utilized from external sources like the government. Even internally, those taking and responding to customer orders may not consider data recording essential tasks. Data recording errors as well as data suitability issues must be considered when reviewing historical data. Often, random, one-time events significantly affect data, and can skew forecasting. Any recordings that are out of the ordinary must be flagged and investigated to verify their suitability for use in the demand forecasting process.

The Role of Outliers, Data Adjustments, and Units of Measure

Outliers are data points that are unusual and of a one-time nature, so they are unlikely to be repeated. When forecasting demand based on past data, it is important to analyze any unusual data to determine the cause and the likelihood of its being repeated. For one-time, unlikely events such as outliers, data can be adjusted or overridden. Overriding or adjusting data is simply leaving out that data which is not indicative of future behavior. The units of measure used in recording order and shipment information as well as forecasting demand must be agreed upon and universally understood. The best unit of measure to use is the number of units sold, shipped, forecasted, etc. Although the marketing and finance departments may prefer the dollar amount sold as the measure, this is impractical since the price changes over time and units of sale do not. The number of units sold, shopped, or anticipated to be sold can be easily converted to a current dollar amount as necessary.

Internal and External

The primary internal data sources that are used in forecasting future demand are past orders received and shipments made by the company. This data should be recorded and stored as number of units shipped and sold, rather than as financial values. External data sources for forecasting demand include market surveys and research, market intelligence, and market changes. Market surveys and research entail discovering directly from those who make up the marketplace their opinions of what the market needs and/or wants and their responses to possible new products.

Utilizing market intelligence to forecast demand involves comparison of the theoretical forecast to market intelligence, what is currently known about the market. Foreknowledge of temporary and permanent market changes also aid in tweaking the forecast demand to a more appropriate figure.

Financial Ramifications

The primary costs associated with demand forecasting are the price paid for any software used and the salaries paid to the personnel who produce the forecast. Demand forecasting can be expensive, but not as expensive as poor planning for the future. The absence of good forecasting is expensive. Inaccurate demand forecasting can cause shortages of necessary items, overstocks of unnecessary items, lost sales, and poor customer service. The finance department should be able to estimate the cost of poor forecasting as well as the savings to be made with good forecasting, so informed decisions about forecast spending can be made.

Methods of Selecting a Demand Forecast

The best demand forecasting method is one that is appropriate for the particular situation, can be understood and therefore used effectively by the responsible personnel, and is cost effective in the specific application. Evaluating the possible methods or systems for complexity as well as how they measure up against each other and against the situation requirements are good selection tools. Past experience can be a gauge, but should not be a limitation. Establishing a clear budget as well as system requirements agreed upon by management and forecasting personnel can make the decision-making process smoother and more effective.

Responsible Personnel

Without prioritization of demand forecasting and clear, assigned responsibility for it, there is no forecast accuracy. Prioritization is important because staff will not work hard to do a good job on an assignment that is not considered important and useful. Clear, assigned responsibility is important because it provides accountability, which in turn provides accuracy. Responsibility for demand forecasting rests nationally with the marketing function, and locally with the sales force. Marketing personnel use mathematical methods based on historical data and market trends to generate a national forecast. The sales personnel base local forecasts on their relationships and communications with current and potential customers. The national marketing and local sales functions must combine their respective forecasts into one, unified forecast that is national and local in scope. Demand forecasting is an ongoing activity, continually checked against actual sales and adjusted accordingly.

Manufacturing Environments and Service Industries

In project manufacturing environments, where each project is unique and handled individually by a project team, forecasting is used in the earlier stages of the project to project the amount of manufacturing capacity required so that capacity can be reserved and available for the project.

In process manufacturing environments, forecasting functions similarly to make-to-stock environments. The product demand is forecast individually and by product family, and replenished as needed so that the number in stock matches the forecast.

In service industries, forecasting involves projecting the amount of resources that will be necessary in the future based on current projects that will extend into the future, potential projects that may materialize, and general market knowledge.

TIME HORIZON

Time horizon – The length of time into the future over which the demand forecast extends; the time horizon can also be called the forecast horizon.

LONG-TERM FORECAST

Long-term forecast – A loose quarterly demand forecast that extends more than two years into the future; the long-term forecast is used to plan for major changes in production capacity, such as additional buildings or capital equipment or expansion of the workforce or financial base; if the long-term forecast does not extend far enough into the future, major changes cannot be accomplished in time to meet demand.

SHORT-TERM FORECAST

Short-term forecast – A reasonably accurate demand forecast that is usually set by the local sales force based on their communication with customers and knowledge of competitors; the short-term forecast is used to set production schedules and finished goods and distribution stock numbers; the time horizon for a short-term forecast is up to three months.

MEDIUM-TERM FORECAST

Medium-term forecast – A demand forecast that is developed from the current long-term and short-term forecasts and used for material planning purposes; having the necessary materials available for manufacturing depends on the medium-term forecast; the accuracy of the medium-term forecast depends on the economy and any changes it experiences; the time horizon for a medium-term forecast can be from three months up to two years.

AGGREGATE AND DISAGGREGATE FORECASTING

The marketing function typically sets the national forecast at the product family or brand name level, which is an aggregate forecast. This aggregate forecast is then used to set production rates and determine labor requirements. It drives the production process. This aggregate forecast is then broken down or disaggregated into individual product forecasts in conjunction with regional sales personnel who are in touch with the customers and potential customers. This single-item or disaggregate forecast is then used to establish distribution center stock requirements. It drives the distribution requirements planning (DRP) system.

TYPES OF DEMAND

Known demand refers to actual future customer needs for products that are already factually known. This includes orders that have been placed but not yet filled and future, scheduled orders. Other known demands can include MRP calculations of dependent demand once a forecast demand has been established for the corresponding independent demand and demands for time and capacity from other departments, such as research, development, engineering, and testing. Forecast demand is unknown, estimated future demand. It is calculated based on historical data or expected future trends, while known demand is factual. True demand is the most difficult type of demand to ascertain. The true demand is the demand that is actually experienced by the company, but for which the company must be prepared beforehand. It is greater than the known demand, but not the same as the known and forecast demand put together.

Promotional demand is the demand for products and/or services that a company experiences in preparation for and in response to a promotion or sale. Disadvantages associated with promotions include the low cost, which is not always tenable for the company, especially if they must increase capacity to meet the demand, and possible decreased demand for other products or for the same product in future periods since customers stock up at the time of the sale (variable vs. level demand). Advantages of promotions can be to increase market share and to adversely affect the competition, as well as to positively impact customer relations.

In addition to the material and capacity demand generated by the master production schedule (MPS) to meet external sales demand, there are internal demands generated by the research, development, engineering, and testing functions. These functions require both material and production capacity to fulfill their responsibilities and obligations. If this internal demand is not accepted and planned for, it can seriously hamper scheduled production. Internal departments must be required to forecast their own demands for goods and capacity, and these demands must be incorporated into the manufacturing plan so that all demands, both internal and external, can be met on schedule.

Demand Forecasting Techniques

Qualitative techniques – Methods of demand forecasting that rely primarily on individual judgment and should be used in combination with less subjective techniques; expert judgment, the Delphi method, market research, management estimation, and historical analogy are all qualitative demand forecasting techniques.

Delphi method – A qualitative demand forecasting technique in which a group of experts is presented with a set of questions related to future demand; each expert answers the questions, and then numerically evaluates the likelihood of occurrence of their peers' answers; the evaluation of the combined list occurs three times, with lower rated answers being removed each time; the final condensed list is used as a basis for long-term or new product forecasting.

Market research – A qualitative demand forecasting technique based on the collection and analysis of information related to marketing products and services, by businesses, external agencies, or their designees, including market analysis, sales analysis, and consumer research.

Market analysis – A form of market research that involves the study of the marketplace itself, such as the number, location, and qualities of the potential customer groups.

Sales analysis – A form of market research that involves the study of sales figures to determine trends and make comparisons.

Consumer research – A form of market research that involves the study of the thoughts, feelings, and other feedback of customers of a particular industry toward that industry's products.

Expert judgment – A qualitative demand forecasting technique in which a group of individuals work together as a team to predict future demand; expert judgment should be used together with one of the intrinsic quantitative methods when possible.

Management estimation – A qualitative demand forecasting technique in which management predictions are based on the instinct of the manager making the prediction; management estimation can be a good feasibility check for more quantitative forecasting methods.

Historical analogy –A qualitative demand forecasting technique used in the case of new products in which historical demand for similar products is used to predict the demand patterns for the short-term until the product builds a sales history of its own.

Intrinsic techniques – Demand forecasting techniques based on internal rather than external data.

Quantitative techniques – Demand forecasting techniques in which forecasts are calculated from data rather than based in personal opinion or expertise.

Simple average – An intrinsic, quantitative demand forecasting technique in which the demand for the next period is determined by averaging the forecast and actual demands for the last period; demand = (demand forecast for the last period + actual demand for the last period)/2.

Year-to-date average – An intrinsic, quantitative demand forecast technique in which the actual demands experienced for the periods during that year are averaged together to determine the forecast demand for the next period of the year; demand = (sum of demands experienced for the year)/(number of periods).

Moving average – An intrinsic, quantitative demand forecast technique in which the forecast demand is calculated by averaging the actual demand over the previous given number of set periods; demand = (sum of demands experienced over the given number of set periods)/(the given number of set periods).

Weighted average – An intrinsic, quantitative demand forecast technique in which the forecast demand is determined by proportionally averaging the forecast and actual demands experienced in the previous period; the proportions assigned must add up to 1 or 100%; demand = (P*forecast)+((1-P)*actual)], where P is the proportion assigned to the previous demand forecast.

Extrinsic techniques – Demand forecasting methods based on external rather than internal data.

Regression – An extrinsic, quantitative demand forecasting technique in which the best mathematical formula to describe the relationship between one or more independent variables and the resulting demand is determined.

Leading indicators – An extrinsic, quantitative demand forecasting method in which relationships between seemingly unrelated events and product demand are observed and used to gauge future demand, such as one type of demand or market indicator creating demand in a different industry; leading indicators can often be followed through governmental statistics.

Econometric models – An extrinsic, quantitative demand forecasting method consisting of groups of equations that govern the interrelationships of dependent, like demand, and independent economic factors.

Single-level, exponential smoothing technique - An intrinsic, quantitative demand forecasting technique. It is a weighted moving average, in which the new forecast is determined by the relationship between old forecasts and actual corresponding demands, proportioned by the age of the data. In first order smoothing, only the most recent time period is considered, and the new forecast is determined by adding a proportion of the difference between the old forecast and the actual demand to the old forecast. The proportion, also called alpha or the smoothing constant, is a management decision and should always be less than 0.5. Alpha should be low when actual demand is erratic and high when actual demand is steady. The new forecast demand using first order smoothing is calculated as follows: demand = old forecast + [alpha*(actual demand – old forecast)].

Time series decomposition - An intrinsic, quantitative demand forecasting technique. The premise of time series decomposition is the observance and recording of actual product sales over an extended period of time (several manufacturing time periods) in order to establish ongoing demand patterns. It is best to use between two and five years of data, so this method is for current established products. Usual patterns observed include level, cyclic, irregular, trends, and seasonal.

Once demand patterns have been observed, they can be projected into the future to form the basis of demand forecasting. The demand forecasts must also be adjusted for seasonality, which can be taken into account through the use of a seasonal index or base series.

Seasonal index - a number based on past seasonality used to adjust demand forecasts for seasonality in the future. The historical average demand is determined, and then the proportion of the average demand (the seasonal index) that was experienced in individual time periods is calculated and used to adjust the demand forecast for corresponding future time periods. The sum of the seasonal indices used should equal the number of time periods considered .A base series is a set of factors indicating the demand over time in a seasonal cycle, based on past demand. The average of the factors in the series is one, and factors greater than one indicate higher than average demand for the time period, while factors less than one indicate less than average demand for the time period. To predict seasonal demand, the base series is combined with the average forecast demand and/or demand trend for the product being forecasted.

Business Cycle Management

Although understanding the general shape and pattern of the business cycle is simple, predicting the actual lengths and magnitudes of the troughs, expansions, peaks, and contractions is challenging. Good prediction of these numbers is crucial to proper forecasting and effective management. Management must plan and prepare for the business cycle stages in advance or risk having too little cash reserve to support the expansion in preparation for the peak, too little finished goods inventory to maximize the peak, too much stock during the contraction following the peak, or other similar problems.

Business Cycle Terms

Business cycle – Business patterns recorded over a period of years in which troughs, expansions, peaks, and contractions are observed and relationships between industries and businesses can be pinpointed.

Trough – The low point of the business cycle in which sales are lowest and cash reserves are highest; the trough is the time to prepare for future expansion.

Expansion – The growth period of the business cycle following the trough in which purchasing, receiving, and stock levels of raw materials, components, work in process, and finished goods increase and cash reserves decrease pending payment for goods produced.

Peak – The highest point of the business cycle following expansion in which sales plateau; in the peak time, material purchases and production should be cut back in preparation for the contraction to follow.

Contraction – The shrinking period of the business cycle in which sales decline from the peak to the trough and material purchases and stock held should continue to decrease while cash held increases as payment comes in for goods sold during the peak time.

Forecast Variance

Since a forecast is simply a prediction of future demand, a certain amount of discrepancy between the forecast demand and the actual demand is to be expected, and since forecast demands are typically averages, there will be ups and downs in demand around those averages even for a good forecast. Forecast variance is the name used for the discrepancies between forecast and actual demands. When there is a consistent forecast variance in one direction that builds cumulatively over time, there is a forecast error or forecast bias that needs to be addressed. Error measurements are used to track forecast variances and monitor for forecast errors or biases. The primary methods of measuring forecast accuracy are the standard deviation and the mean absolute deviation (MAD).

Analyzing Demand History

Recording historical demand patterns is an important step in demand forecasting. Once a thorough historical record of demand over time is available, it can be analyzed and utilized for management decisions. Fundamentally, the average demand for past time periods can be calculated, and then followed by more detailed analysis. The first step is to establish the demand bands. This is done by determining the range of demand experienced and dividing that range into discrete bands for categorization. The second step is to categorize the demand experienced in the past time periods into their appropriate demand bands. The third step is to count the demand density experienced per band. Finally, the cumulative percentage demand experienced per demand band is calculated and recorded.

The analysis of demand history serves as a tool for management decision-making, particularly in determining the amount of safety stock to hold. The analysis makes clear what percentage of past demand could be filled successfully at varying stock levels. For example, if the demand range maximum was held in stock at all times, then it is probable that all demands could be met from stock at all times, but consistently holding the maximum historical demand in stock is not a feasible solution. From the analysis, management can see what percentage of demand can be successfully met at varying stock levels. Although this is a useful management tool for determining safety stock, it is not the only safety stock consideration.

When the number of occurrences of historical demand per demand band is plotted graphically, the result is typically assumed to be the normal distribution curve, or the bell curve, although other distributions are possible. In the normal distribution, most of the demands experienced will be close to the mean demand, and few will be far from the mean, resulting in the familiar bell curve. A narrower bell curve shows fewer variations from the mean, while a wider bell curve shows more variations from the mean. The normal distribution for a demand analysis can be summarized with two numbers – the mean and the standard deviation of historical demand.

The mean demand is the average of the historical demands experienced. The mean demand is calculated by summing together the historical demands being considered and dividing the sum by the number of historical demands being considered. In relation to the normal distribution curve, the mean demand is the average of the curve values (in this case, demand) and is the midpoint of the curve. The portions of the curve before and after the mean should be equal mirror images. The mean demand is a very useful figure commonly used in many applications.

The standard deviation is a measurement of the spread or flatness of the particular normal distribution in question. In the case of analyzing historical demand data for forecast error, it is a measure of the variation experienced in the historical demand. In the normal distribution curve, which can be defined by the mean and the standard deviation, there are three standard deviations before and three standard deviations after the mean or midpoint of the curve. The standard deviation is typically symbolically represented by the Greek symbol sigma, and is calculated by taking the sum of the squares of the individual deviations between actual and forecast demands, dividing by the number of historical periods considered, and taking the square root.

The mean absolute deviation (MAD) is analogous to the standard deviation. In fact, the MAD was used historically to calculate an approximation of the standard deviation using the formula standard deviation = 1.25 * MAD, since the calculation is simpler and early computers were challenged by the complexity of calculating the standard deviation. Like standard deviation, the

MAD is a measure of the variation experienced in the historical demand pattern. The MAD is calculated by taking the sum of the absolute deviations between actual and forecast historical demands and dividing by the number of periods considered.

When the forecast demand is held in stock, stock-outs do not occur as long as the actual demand is equal to or less than the forecast. When the actual demand exceeds the forecast, a stock-out occurs. When holding only the forecast demand in stock, fifty percent of demands can typically be met from stock. It has been statistically shown that if one additional standard deviation of historical demand is held, then demands experienced up to 34% above the average, or 84% of all demands, can be met from stock. If two extra standard deviations are held, 97.7% of demands can be met from stock, and for three extra standard deviations held 99.9% of demands can be met from stock. It can be seen that with the increasing number of extra standard deviations held in stock the percentage of actual demands met will increase, but not proportionately. The gain from the second standard deviation is conspicuously less significant than from the first, and the gain from the third even less so.

Forecast Monitoring Terms

Magnitude – The extent of the discrepancies between the actual demand and the forecast demand values.

Variability – The full range of actual demand values experienced, from minimum to maximum.

Bias – Consistent variability between the actual demand and forecast demand values in the same direction, indicating a consistent problem in the forecasting that needs addressing.

Outlier – A one-of-a-kind, out-of-the-ordinary, non-reproducible actual demand value warranting special investigation and exclusion from the historical data set used to forecast product demand.

Timing – Time variability within the overall sales pattern that does not affect the totals.

Product Life Cycle Stages

<u>Pre-product development</u> – Research and development based not on specific products but on more general ideas like the properties and capabilities of materials which ultimately allow for the development of new products; since the product has not even been identified yet, demand forecasting does not play a role in pre-product development.

<u>Product development</u> – The development of potential new products, prior to any formalized production or even decision to go forward with the product; in product development, the role of demand forecasting is to investigate the likely market acceptance level and lifespan of the product to help determine if development should continue.

<u>Testing and introduction</u> – The product life cycle stage in which standards for the product are established and fulfilled; the role of demand forecasting during testing and introduction is market research, comparison to similar historical projects, if available, and statistical tracking of early sales in order to ascertain the probable short-term and long-term demand.

<u>Rapid growth</u> – The full launch of the product into the marketplace, with the corresponding increase in sales; the role of demand forecasting during rapid growth is to use market research, relevant historical data, and sales results from the testing and introduction stage to determine the demand forecast which must be met so that manufacturing can be structured accordingly.

<u>Steady state</u> – Consistent trends or seasons in sales reached after the rapid growth stage that can be effectively forecast through historical data and market research in order to meet demand.

Phasing out – The end of the manufacture and sale of a product, either through a gradual decline or a rapid end due to replacement; demand forecasting is used in the phasing out process to predict the declining sales, determine the point at which manufacturing is no longer profitable, and establish demand and demand time horizon for service parts.

Ordering Process

Assemble- and Make-to-Order Production

In an assemble-to-order production environment, the master production schedule is based on modules rather than finished goods, since the actual finished goods to be produced must be specified by the customer. As part of the ordering process, the customer must specify the options they want in their product. This often involves a configuration module in the order entry system that prompts the order personnel for the choices made by the customer. With use of the configuration module, the customer service representative cannot skip any necessary configuration information, and the order promise date is calculated automatically based on the options chosen.

In a make-to-order production environment, the item is not manufactured at all until the customer order is received. If the order is for a standard item, then a price and lead time can be quoted immediately. For non-standard items, a price must be estimated from material and labor costs and lead time must be estimated based on material and capacity availability.

Engineer-to-Order, Project, and Process Production

The engineer-to-order production environment is similar to the make-to-order production environment; with the primary difference that engineer-to-order includes a design stage. For typical items, the cost and lead time of manufacture, including design work, is already known and can be quoted to the customer. For out-of-the-ordinary items, price and lead time estimation is performed and checked with the customer as part of the design process .In a project production environment, detailed discussion with the customer is necessary, which is then followed by an in-depth proposal for the project including the price.

Process industries usually function similarly to make-to-stock production environments, so the order entry process is simple and straightforward. Finished goods are stocked according to a demand forecast, and orders received are filled from stock.

Customer Orders

Off-the-shelf order – A customer order made and received based on the assumption that the item is consistently in inventory and can thus be filled from stock; the inventory is stocked according to a demand forecast.

Advance order – A customer order made for large quantities to be delivered in the future at time(s) yet to be specified through product call-offs; the customer reaps the economic advantage usually associated with large order quantities, and the manufacturer has a general idea of future demand related to that customer although it has not yet been specifically stated; the manufacturer is promising the customer items to be produced in the future rather than items currently in stock.

Customized order – A customer order for a product that is not currently available since specialization is required in order for the product to meet customer requirements, as is the case in engineer-to-order, make-to-order, assemble-to-order, and package-to-order production environments.

SPECIAL ORDERS

Spare part order – A customer order for spare parts or service parts necessary for maintenance or repair of the original product; spare part orders can be considered a service since they are not the primary item produced by the manufacturer and because of the short turn-around time generally associated with them.

Intra-company demand – Orders received from other companies within a group of companies or other divisions within the same company; intra-company orders are usually handled according to the regular order-handling procedure, and, depending on the operational philosophy, they can be handled as high- or low-priority Interplant demand – Orders received from other companies within a group of companies, other divisions within the same company, or even the same division, but the orders are specifically received from another site, which is not necessarily the case with intra-company demands.

SERVICE ORDERS

Customer orders for services are reservations for a service supplied rather than a product manufactured. Service orders are typically project-based; that is, the order entails the completion of a particular project. Customer service orders can be priced in two ways, at a fixed time rate, such as an hourly or daily charge in effect until the project is completed, or at a project rate, in which one agreed upon price is charged for the completion of the project without regard to the time required, although a time projection is probably factored into the price quoted. Alternatively, the project price can be tied into the measurable results of the project outcome.

ORDER ENTRY

Order entry is the process of receiving communication from customers about what they want and translating that information into the proper terminology, documentation, and company system to trigger the filling of the order. The level of complexity involved varies greatly according to the production environment, from a simple process in a make-to-stock environment to an extremely complex process in a make- or engineer-to-order environment. Successfully meeting customer promise dates for orders depends on the accuracy of the order entry process. Ensuring order entry accuracy requires an order entry system designed to prevent errors and personnel with a proper understanding of the importance of order accuracy.

ORDER-RELATED TERMS

Order entry date – The day on which the initial order is received and accepted, including an agreement for price charged and delivery date of goods.

Customer requested date – The original day on which the customer asks that the goods be delivered, which may or may not be agreed to by the manufacture depending on product availability.

Order promise date – The day on which the manufacturer agrees to deliver the goods, which may or may not be the customer requested date, depending on product availability.

Revised promise date – The day on which the manufacturer commits to deliver the goods ordered if for some reason the original order promise date becomes untenable.

Substitution – The replacement of an ordered item with an alternative item acceptable to the customer when the item requested is not available within the time frame required; substitution often involves upgrading, and whether the customer pays the price difference is a management decision.

Change order – A formal adjustment made to an order that has already been placed but is still being processed; change orders can be triggered by customer requests or internal engineering or inventory changes.

Customer return – The receipt of goods previously ordered by and delivered to a customer back to the manufacturer, often because the item was unacceptable in some way; customer returns are a trigger for investigation internally and with the customer.

Customer Interface Management

Effective customer interface management relies on feasible order delivery commitments and maintenance of positive customer relationships. Feasible order delivery commitments and positive customer relationships can be accomplished through effective communication with customers, appropriate application of customer relationship management (CRM) concepts, establishment and execution of good order handling procedures, and continuous internal analysis and improvement through performance measurements of the order handling system. Measurement and improvement of on-time order delivery performance is especially important. As in any aspect of competing in the marketplace, continuous improvement is required to maintain and increase market share.

Customer Service

CRM

Customer relationship management (CRM) is a business and marketing strategy in which the customer is the central consideration. CRM is accomplished through improvement in every aspect of customer service, including fast and effective order entry, on time and accurate delivery, and responsiveness to customer needs and requests. CRM includes obtaining feedback from customers to further improve service. The ultimate goal of CRM is the development of lifetime customers through building long-term relationships that are beneficial to both manufacturers and their customers. Lifetime customers are important because maintenance of current customers is less expensive than finding new ones, long-term customer relationships result in manufacturers' better understanding and meeting customer needs, and repeat business and referrals from current customers due to faithful service.

CRM Environment

Product – The goods being sold, along with the supporting services which are tailored specifically to individual customers.

Price – The cost for goods charged by the manufacturer; the price must be profitable for the manufacturer as well as appealing to the customers, and is based on customer relationships, market competition, and order-winning strategy.

Placement – The presentation and availability of the product to the customer, as well as customer education, service, and support available for the product.

Promotion – The act of keeping the product in view of potential customers to create demand for the product through advertising, sales, public relations, and publicity, with policies set individually for the customer(s) being targeted, rather than a general audience.

Customer-Focused Organization

The first step in becoming a customer-focused organization is to change the business philosophy. Thinking must change at every level of the organization from a product focus to a customer focus. The second step is to better serve the customers by identifying their needs, both generally and individually. The third step is to create customer maps for each customer, including their identities, strategies, and policies, and how to approach them and work with them most effectively. The fourth step is implementation of the customer relationship management (CRM) program. This is the actual execution of the plans made from the customer information with the new customer focus. The fifth and final step of becoming a customer-focused organization is continuous improvement. The business must continually examine itself and its customer satisfaction levels with the goal of improvement.

ORDER DELIVERY PERFORMANCE

Measuring order delivery performance is an important step in customer service improvement. For many customers, a reliable promise date, or the supplier's ability to deliver the ordered products when promised, is more important than a quick delivery date, although a quick promise date can also provide competitive edge if it is met. Delivery performance measurement can be considered from three standpoints: how a company ranks as a customer to their suppliers, how a company ranks as a supplier to their customers, and to what extent a company meets its order winners and qualifiers. Some specific examples of order delivery performance measurements include the percentage of on-time deliveries, the percentage of orders shipped within the target date, the percentage of deliveries with no problems reported, the number or percentage of customer orders not accepted, the number of orders delivered early, the number or percentage of orders with internal handling problems, and the number or percentage of orders not met from stock in a make-to-stock production environment.

SUPPLIER FEEDBACK

The role of supplier feedback, although indirect, can be a key component in customer service. As a company gets what they need when they need it from their suppliers, the company is better able to meet the needs of their own customers. The key to good supplier relationships, to being a good customer, is open communication. As a company receives feedback from and provides feedback to their suppliers, the relationship is strengthened and mutually benefits both parties. Communication of details such as how much lead time is necessary for order processing from the supplier to the customer and the customer's exact preferences and requirements in material and service enable better service in both directions.

CUSTOMER FEEDBACK

Customer feedback is a crucial and direct element in customer service. It is through knowing what the customers want from and think of a company that the company can actually improve its performance. There are two ways that customer feedback can work. The first way is through the company's own initiative, using tools like questionnaires, surveys, follow-up phone calls, and more. Customer feedback can also occur through the customer's initiative, like voluntary product complaints or commendations, and more formally through supplier feedback systems. In order to successfully meet customer desires and expectations, companies must know what those desires and expectations are and to what extent they are meeting them.

SUPPLIER RATINGS SYSTEMS

Supplier rating systems are formal procedures whereby customers rate their suppliers in terms of performance. These rating systems are highly specific to individual customers, and are dependent on the industry, company, and production environment under consideration. Companies establish their own priorities for their suppliers and rate them accordingly. Historically, low cost and on-time delivery were considered of ultimate importance. As manufacturing has changed over time, quality and responsiveness have emerged as significant factors. Ultimately, each company is unique and has their own requirements for their suppliers; requirements that their suppliers need to know in order to supply the company successfully in the long term. Open communication between the customer and supplier regarding the supplier's performance according to the customer's rating system is essential in closing the loop and making the rating system an effective tool in improving service.

Internal Performance Measurements

Although supplier feedback, customer feedback, and customer supplier rating systems are crucial steps toward improved customer service, they do not replace or negate the need for a company's own internal performance measurements. Traditionally, internal performance measurements have been financial in nature, but these are not necessarily the most effective since they tend to encourage overproduction. The current trend in manufacturing is the use of performance measurements that encourage performance to plan. The traditional financial measurements are being augmented or replaced by manufacturing and other measurements related to quality, work force skill sets, and adherence to plan.

Manufacturing Performance

Manufacturing is the foundation of customer service. Without the successful manufacture of products, there are no goods to sell to the customers, and thus no customer service. Beyond the successful manufacture of goods, customer service relies on the manufacture of goods according to schedule, which can be tracked and improved. Manufacturing performance can be tracked at three levels: adherence to sales and operations planning schedules, adherence to master schedules, and adherence to shop schedules. Sales and operations planning schedules specify the overall quantities of product families to be manufactured per time period, usually monthly. Master schedules specify the quantities of products and/or modules to be manufactured per shortened time period, daily or weekly. Shop schedules, usually in the form of daily dispatch lists, specify the jobs to be performed by workstation per day. All of these levels can be measured by percentage of completion to schedule, and improvements made accordingly to improve customer service.

Manufacturing Performance Measurements

At the sales and operations planning level of manufacturing, the monthly percentage complete of planned production of product families can serve as a customer service improvement indicator.

At the master scheduling level, the weekly or daily percentage complete of planned production of products or product modules, the weekly or daily percentage complete of planned final assembly of goods, the number of changes made to the master schedule, the percentage of order promise dates met successfully the first time, and the number of changed delivery promise dates can all serve as customer service improvement indicators. At the shop performance level, the number of skill sets developed by production workers, the number of hours of unplanned overtime, the number of hours of unplanned subcontract time or the number of unplanned subcontract orders, and the number of hours of expedited work can all service as customer service improvement indicators.

Non-Manufacturing Performance

In addition to the critical role of manufacturing performance in customer service, non-manufacturing performance is also important. Some specific examples of non-manufacturing performance indicators that play important roles in customer service include forecast accuracy, customer service itself, on-time shipment and delivery, and customer returns. Forecast accuracy can be measured by tracking and comparing demand forecasts to the actual orders received. Customer service can be measured by the percentage of orders, order line items, or order dollar amounts met delivered on time, or fulfilled from stock. Timeliness of shipment and delivery is measured simply by tracking the number or percentage of orders shipped or delivered by the original order promise date, and secondarily the number or percentage of orders shipped or delivered by their renegotiated order promise date. Finally, customer returns are tracked by monitoring the number of orders returned by customers as well as the reason for the returns. If analyzed and used properly to spur improvements, all of these performance measurements can contribute greatly to customer service.

Churning

Churning is the movement of customers from their current suppliers to new suppliers that are perceived to be better in some way, such as lower price, better service, or higher quality. The goal of customer relationship management (CRM) is the development of long-term customer relationships, which is the opposite of churning, so good CRM prevents churning. More specifically, the CRM process should include in-depth, ongoing analysis of current customers, including indications of vulnerability to churning so that specific action can be taken to prevent this eventuality in the cases of at-risk customers.

Performance Targets

The primary consideration in setting effective performance targets is the human reaction to them. The targets set must encourage personnel to meet company objectives through performance to the company plan. Traditionally, performance targets have focused on production rather than sales through such performance measures as machine utilization, but this leads to waste. Unnecessary production hinders continuity between company objectives and employee performance. The goal is to meet the plan, which entails successfully meeting sales goals, not producing as much as possible. In addition to encouraging workers to act according to company goals, performance targets should be realistic and measurable. When the goal to be reached is distant from the current situation, more manageable short-term goals should be set, met, and rewarded so that employees do not grow discouraged and give up because the goal seems impossible. Some performance measurements include percentage of on-time deliveries, number of stock-outs, number of orders processed, number of orders not processed on the day received, number of customer returns, and record accuracy.

Benchmarking

The purpose of benchmark measurements is to understand the level of improvement that is feasible and/or necessary. Typically, benchmark measurements are based on comparison of a product, process, or company to its competitors or the industry standard. Benchmark measurements occur before changes are undertaken to establish the end goal of the change. Special care must be taken to ensure that the comparisons made in benchmarking are valid. For benchmarking to be valid, the manufacturing situations being compared must manufacture from the same level under comparable operating conditions, which is not always or even often the case.

CPI

Continuous process improvement (CPI) is the ongoing process of eliminating waste and solving problems in the production process. Waste is anything that is unnecessary, and solving problems entails identifying and eliminating the root causes, not simply coping. Both managers and workers are involved, and improvements tend to be small rather than large. CPI can be accomplished in two ways, either by better executing and solving problems within the existing process through tools like control charts or by changing the process itself. The first approach lends itself to small, ongoing changes while the second lends itself to major, one-time changes. The biggest obstacle to CPI is resistance to change. An atmosphere of ongoing improvement must be purposefully created so that employees will continually make suggestions. CPI is also referred to as kaizen, the Japanese term for improvement.

CTP

The term capable-to-promise (CTP) refers to the availability of material, capacity, and other resources to provide goods within a specified quantity and time frame. It is the capability of the company to commit to a particular customer request at a given time.

ATP

The term available-to-promise (ATP) refers to the facility within the master scheduling function that combines information such as current inventory, manufacturing schedule, forecast customer orders, and current customer orders to determine if the company has or will have CTP goods available within a customer-specified quantity and time frame. Using the ATP facility or tool, sales representatives can commit to customer requests, or make alternative suggestions if the customer's request is not possible. The success of the ATP tool depends on current and accurate record keeping as well as realistic manufacturing schedules.

EDI

Electronic data interchange (EDI) is the paperless transfer of information between company computer systems, using a standardized data format. Purchase orders, shipment authorizations, shipment notices, and invoices are all examples of documents that are transmitted via EDI between suppliers and their customers, making the flow of information instantaneous and saving significant time and effort over physical delivery.

With the use of EDI, the quality and speed of information flow increases which keeps everyone involved aware of changes, eases the process of kanban and release ordering systems, and shortens lead times. EDI is a dedicated, specially installed system used between the parties involved.

INTERNET

The internet is a worldwide exchange of information through the World Wide Web, e-mail, and other applications powered by a global computer network formed through connecting individual computers and computer systems with telecommunications hardware. The internet provides a general electronic connection between suppliers and customers, unlike electronic data exchange (EDI), which is specific to the supplier-customer relationship in question. The internet can be used for instantaneous worldwide messaging (e-mail), publishing the availability of products and services, and acceptance of customer orders and payments. Through the internet, customer-supplier transactions can occur instantaneously, at any time, and without any vocal or face-to-face contact.

PLANNER-TO-PLANNER COMMUNICATION

In the past, all customer-supplier communication took place between the buyers and salesmen for the respective companies. This involved unnecessary time and people when it came to sorting out actual deliveries and manufacturing changes. Today, the salesmen and buyers typically make the initial agreement between the two companies including pricing and basic contract stipulations, but the specifics as to what should be delivered when, how to handle changes that arise, and the overall material flow are handled by the company planners. The improved effectiveness of communication when planners instead of buyers and salesman handle material flow is especially apparent in accommodating last-minute changes and urgent requests.

COMMITTING GOODS

Making commitments to customers to either ship or deliver goods is called order promising. In make-to-order production environments, order promising involves first checking the available materials and capacity with which the product can be assembled. In make-to-stock production environments, order promising involves checking the available goods in inventory and scheduled to be manufactured. Companies can check availability in two ways. The most reliable is using the available-to-promise (ATP) facility within the master scheduling module. If this system is not in use, order promising is typically based on the product lead time. As long as there is sufficient time between making the promise and the delivery or shipment date to assemble the product, it is assumed that the promise can be made and met. The possibilities of over scheduling or material shortages are not considered. From this it can be seen that the ATP facility, when implemented appropriately, provides significant customer service improvement.

Promise Date Renegotiation

When a company has missed their promise date to the customer, they enter the process of promise date renegotiation. This is determining in conjunction with the internal sales, marketing, and manufacturing departments as well as the customer what the new promise date will be. As important as it is to meet promise dates, it is even more important to meet renegotiated promise dates. Meeting promise dates and renegotiated promise dates is especially important when the customer is a manufacturer since their production process relies on the materials supplied.

Customer-Requested Change

Customer-requested changes can involve both date and quantity adjustments. In make-to-stock production environments these changes can be simple, as long as stock is available to meet demand and order processing has not already begun. In make-to-order environments, change orders can be more complex. In all cases, it is best to meet the customer's needs if possible, using tools like expediting when necessary. A company's ability to meet the customer's changing needs is a measure of their responsiveness.

Delay and Early Shipment Notification

When a company realizes that a shipment will be made before or after the promise date, they should notify the customer of the change immediately. For customers who plan shipments exactly to meet demand and unload directly to the manufacturing line without a storage interval, a shipment date change can be quite inconvenient, but can be handled better if is planned for rather than unexpected.

The basic stages of an order, or the order statuses, are initial customer inquiry, quotation, order placement, confirmation, order handling, delivery, invoicing, and completion. If the goods are manufactured after the order is received, manufacturing stages may also be documented as order statuses. Keeping track of the order and its current status is part of customer service. Customers may seek confirmation of the delivery date, which requires order status tracking to verify that the steps are proceeding on target to meet the deadline.

Distribution Planning

Distribution Management

Distribution management is a critical component of the total supply chain. A company with excellent purchasing and manufacturing but with troublesome distribution is a company with problems. The supply chain is not complete until the customer receives their goods, preferably on the promise date. The distribution system must be wholly integrated into the company, with functions such as order promising, order handling, and physical delivery of the product. The two primary systems used for replenishing stock at distribution centers are the pull system, based on decentralized control, and the push system, based on centralized control.

DECENTRALIZED CONTROL

One of the chief goals of distribution planning is to use efficient administrative controls to achieve a high level of customer service within a cost ceiling. Decentralized control of materials inventory distribution is one of two distinct and different policy measures to achieve this.

The manager of a decentralized distribution chain operates independently. Such a manager is responsible for all the customers within the area or distribution network. The central distribution warehouse is run as if it is a separate business.

Decentralized control assumes that stock is always available for replenishment. The manager employing this distribution method uses a stock replenishment plan based on time or stock level inventories. In other words, the manager sets reordering points according to weeks, months, or other time intervals, or by developing a system that will trigger reordering when a specific inventory count is reached.

PULL SYSTEM

Pull system, or decentralized distribution control, is a distribution control system in which each distribution center is run somewhat independently. The distribution center manager is responsible for sales made from that distribution center and for maintaining the stock to meet those sales, which is typically done using the traditional reorder point method or the periodic review method to replenish stock from the central warehouse. Advantages of the pull system include autonomy for the individual distribution centers and lower communication costs due to autonomy. Disadvantages of the pull system are the lack of coordination of demands on the central warehouse from the individual distribution centers, the rudimentary methods of stock replenishment in use at the distribution centers leaving them vulnerable to stock-outs when the appropriate conditions are not met, and the lack of transferability of stock from one distribution center to another.

PUSH SYSTEM

The push system, or centralized distribution control, is a distribution control system in which the individual distribution center managers are responsible to forecast their future demands and the planner at the central warehouse coordinates distribution requirements planning to supply the central warehouse and the individual distribution centers accordingly. Advantages of the push system include the overall and future planning aspects rather than the reaction to individual demands prevalent in the pull system, the resulting ability to coordinate manufacturing with the distribution demand, the transferability of stock between distribution centers as appropriate due to centralized planning, and the ease of implementation of new policies. Disadvantages of the push system include higher communication costs and the physical separation between what is actually happening at individual distribution centers and the decision making affecting those distribution centers.

DISTRIBUTION NETWORKS

Distribution networks are utilized when companies opt to store their finished goods inventory in more than one location in order to provide quick deliveries to customers in more than one geographic area. The central warehouse distributes goods to the regional warehouses, which in turn distribute goods to the customers. Some factors to consider in planning distribution networks include the locations, size, replenishment method, systems support, and volume of stock held for the individual sites. Distribution networks can become complex as greater geographic areas are served. In some cases, the factory supplies the central warehouse, the central warehouse supplies regional warehouses, and the regional warehouses supply the local customers. It is also possible for multiple factories to supply the distribution network.

INVENTORY STOCKING POLICY

The goal of a company's distribution network as well as its related inventory stocking policy is to provide the customer service level required in an economically feasible manner. Distribution networks are typically associated with make-to-stock production companies. A make-to-stock company can also use its distribution network to deliver make-to-order and expensive, lower-demand items, but these items will not likely be stored within the distribution network. The inventory stocking policy entails the quantity of safety stock to be held, the order quantity, and the stock replenishment frequency. The required customer service level sets the safety stock quantity, and the replenishment frequency sets the order quantity. The average stock held in a warehouse is its safety stock plus half of its order quantity.

LEAD TIME

The purpose of a distribution network is to locate material closer to customers so that delivery time is quicker. This, in essence, provides a shorter order handling and delivery lead time for the customer, which can be crucial to customer service. The time that the material spends in transit is a consideration for the manufacturer, however. Time spent in transit is still time in inventory, which involves costly holding and transport costs, especially in the bulk transit often employed to move material from the central warehouse to the distribution centers. Considering the cost of holding inventory unnecessarily, even in transit, it can be cheaper for the manufacturer to use faster, more expensive modes of transportation for goods.

SAFETY STOCK

The standard safety stock calculation assumes that there is one supply of goods available for sale to customers, which is not the case in a distribution network. The general rule regarding safety stock applied in distribution networks is not to keep safety stock in more than one place for the same customers. Safety stock can be held solely at the central warehouse if deliveries are made to distribution centers daily, but should be kept at the distribution centers if deliveries are less often or unreliable. When the safety stock is held at the distribution centers, it is not necessary to keep the total standard safety stock at each distribution center, but rather a special safety stock per distribution center is calculated as follows: safety stock per distribution center = standard safety stock / Sqrt (number of distribution centers). The standard safety stock is the quantity of safety stock that would be necessary if all stock divided between the distribution centers was held in one warehouse.

FINANCIAL CONSIDERATIONS

As with any financial decision, the considerations associated with distribution centers are the costs incurred and the benefits reaped. The costs incurred in operating a distribution network include the associated overhead as well as the carrying costs of safety stock. The overhead costs accrued by distribution networks include the staff, building(s), outfitting the building(s), and more. The inventory among the distribution centers should remain the same as if only one central warehouse were used, but the safety stock will increase if it is maintained at the distribution centers instead of at the central warehouse. The benefits reaped from a distribution network include lower transportation costs due to bulk shipping from the central warehouse to the distribution centers as well as nearness to customers, which decreases delivery time and increases responsiveness.

CUSTOMER SERVICE

The overall customer service policy for a distribution network is set by the customer service level agreed upon by upper level management to in the sales and operations planning meeting. This customer service level applies to all aspects of operation. The resulting distribution customer service policy attributes are set as needed within the particular industry, company, and operating environment to provide the required customer service level. Some of these considerations include the nearness to customers, the mode of delivery, tangible and intangible customer service characteristics desired, and the speed of delivery, all as warranted by the context.

LOCATION STRATEGIES

The locations of factories and distribution centers are not random, but rather are determined by financial and/or historical considerations. Both proximity to the supplier as well as proximity to the customer are important considerations. Proximity to the supplier is of special concern when the raw materials utilized in manufacturing are not easily transportable, and proximity to the customer is the primary factor in distribution center location. Alternatively, proximity to a transportation hub can be used to ensure ease of receipt and/or shipment of goods. Local conditions at potential sites are also critical. Factors such as tax concessions or other governmental perks, the availability of the necessary utilities and infrastructure for the production in question, the cost of land and building construction and maintenance, environmental concerns, and the availability, skill sets, and rates of labor can also impact or determine site location decisions.

SHIPMENT SCHEDULING

The primary consideration in the process of scheduling shipments to replenish distribution centers is the volume and frequency of deliveries required. It is a simple matter to schedule frequent, large shipments to high-volume distribution centers. Handling low-volume distribution centers is more complex since there is a trade-off between delivery frequency and size. Larger loads are more economical to ship, but the time required for the distribution center to need a large load increases the safety stock requirement at the distribution center. For frequent deliveries of smaller loads, the safety stock expense is decreased, but transportation costs are increased.

Deliveries to customers should be organized in an efficient manner, typically geographically, in order to avoid waste. Efficient, cost-effective organization of customer deliveries is accomplished through local and long-distance route scheduling. Local route scheduling involves geographic organization, customer requirements, and knowledge of the customers. Long-distance route scheduling involves consideration of weather, most economic mode of transport, drop-off points, and return load. Computer programs are now available for the optimization of route scheduling.

SHIPMENT TRACKING

Shipment tracking is the concept of knowing where any particular shipment is at any given time during the delivery process. Technological advances have made this facility possible and even feasible. In most cases, shipment tracking is not required unless there is a problem. For a smooth delivery, simple proof of delivery is usually enough. Once a problem occurs with a shipment, such as not being delivered on schedule, shipment tracking is essential. Specialized delivery services utilize sophisticated technology to track shipments, and some manufacturers even invest internally in sophisticated technology for shipment tracking, depending on the industry and environment.

NUMBER AND LOCATIONS

To determine the most economically effective number and location(s) of distribution centers to be used, a company must first research the distribution costs associated with delivering goods to each area served from each of the potential distribution center sites. Simplistically, the company can decide where to locate the centers geographically and then allocate customers to distribution centers based on the economic data collected. More precisely, the company can determine the cost of distributing goods to all customers from each potential site and select the least expensive site as the primary, and perhaps only, distribution center. Next, the economic feasibility of a second distribution center site is investigated by establishing the cost of using the primary site in combination with each potential additional site to determine if the primary site alone or the primary site in combination with a secondary site is more cost effective, and which secondary site is most cost effective. The research is continued for additional sites until the point of diminishing returns is reached.

Once the number and location(s) of distribution centers are finalized, customers are formally assigned to one of them. After customer allocation, future business at each distribution center can be forecast based on historical information and future predictions. Once the volume of business is known, the frequency and quantity of replenishment shipments, the safety stock quantity, and the necessary distribution center personnel can be calculated to provide the customer service level required.

Size

The size required in a distribution center is determined by the following related factors: the volume of sales and/or deliveries handled through the center, the company's required customer service level, the quantity of safety stock necessary to maintain the desired customer service level, the replenishment order quantities, and the average and maximum stock held, which are determined by the replenishment order quantities. The distribution center must be large enough to accommodate the stock level associated with all of these factors.

Forecasting Demand

Within a distribution network, demand occurs at the distribution centers. In order to meet that demand, the demand must be forecast and the centers stocked accordingly. There are two different methods for forecasting demand for the individual distribution centers in a network. The first is to make a general or national forecast for the whole business, which is then broken down into demand for the individual centers based on the percentage of overall historical demand experienced at each center. This method is based primarily on historical information. The alternative is to forecast the demand for individual items at individual distribution centers, and then reconcile the totals to the national forecast. This method takes future expectations into account.

Order Point Method

The order point method of replenishing distribution center inventory entails monitoring stock levels and ordering a new batch of an item when its stock level reaches the predetermined order point. The amount ordered is fixed, and can either be the economic order quantity (EOQ) or some other fixed quantity. The order point is calculated using the following equation: order point = (demand per time period * order lead time in time periods) + safety stock. The order point system is a traditional replenishment method also known as the variable cycle, fixed order quantity system. The order point system assumes that demand for the item is independent and thus must be forecast, that demand is steady and ongoing, that supplier order promise dates do not change, that stock should always be available for use and should be replenished as it is used, and that long-term planning is not necessary. These assumptions must be met or allowed for in some way if not met for the order point method to be effective.

Disadvantage of the Order Point Inventory

When the order point method of inventory replenishment is used in a distribution network, the individual distribution centers independently handle their own order planning and ordering. There is no orchestration or combined planning of replenishment for the distribution network as a whole. The central warehouse is unaware of the demand until orders for goods are received from the individual distribution centers. Since each center acts independently, it is possible for the central warehouse to be overwhelmed by orders received close together. The result of this combined demand that is above average and unanticipated is a stock-out at the central warehouse and at some distribution centers, an unfortunate situation in which the company would not be able to meet demand until manufacturing catches up with the backlog.

DRP

Distribution requirements planning (DRP) is an inventory replenishment method in which future distribution requirements are predicted and then planned for accordingly. The amount of goods to be shipped from each distribution center is planned, then the steps necessary to have those goods in stock in the centers when required are calculated and performed, all the way back to the central warehouse. DRP is based on meeting projected future requirements, with those requirements determined by the overall company plan and forecast. DRP is analogous to material requirements planning (MRP), and the same logic and rules apply. The time-phased order point method is used at individual distribution centers in conjunction with DRP.

Time-Phased Order Point

The time-phased order point method of inventory replenishment is used at individual distribution centers in conjunction with distribution requirements planning (DRP) for the overall distribution network. With this system, stock in the distribution centers is replenished both as it is used and as future demand requires it. Stock levels are monitored and replenished when they reach their set order point, and inventory is also stocked when current levels are not enough to meet anticipated future demand. Unlike the order point method, the time-phased order point method can be used to successfully stock inventory for changes in demand.

Distribution

Distribution is the link between manufacturing and logistics, as well as between order entry and logistics. Logistics includes functions such as vehicle capacity planning, vehicle loading, vehicle scheduling, vehicle routings, and warehouse receipt planning. Through the use of distribution requirements planning (DRP), the actual customer orders provide the necessary shipment quantities which are then used for shipment planning and the effective use of logistics resources to provide the required customer service level. DRP feeds into and is fed by the master production schedule (MPS), which is fed by material requirements planning (MRP), connecting all of manufacturing to distribution and logistics, all driven by actual customer orders.

Distribution System Performance

Distribution system performance measurements are used to quantify the level of customer service provided by a company, and to make adjustments to improve that customer service level. Inventory record accuracy is a critical performance measurement since it is often problematic. Other distribution performance measurements include the effectiveness of vehicle usage, the performance levels of subcontractors, the accuracy of the sales forecast in comparison to actual sales, the accuracy of standard lead times in comparison to actual lead times, the accuracy of inventory planning figures when compared to actual inventory, the number of inventory stock-outs at the central warehouse, and the level of customer service provided. There are many possible measurements, and each company must decide based on the industry, the company environment, and the company goals which measurements will encourage the desired results.

Distribution Terms

Manufacturing center – The plant at which goods are produced from raw materials and component parts and from which the goods are sent to the plant finished goods inventory or into the distribution network.

Distribution center – A warehouse storing finished goods and service parts for sale and delivery to local customers; distribution centers are also called branch warehouses.

Regional distribution center – A warehouse that stores finished goods and service parts to supply the distribution centers within the geographic area.

Warehouse – A storage facility with the purpose of receiving and storing stock until it is needed by a third party, either a different department within the company or an external customer.

Retailer – A company that sells goods to the final customer after purchasing them from a manufacturer and receiving them from the manufacturer's central warehouse or distribution center.

Bill of distribution – The defined path product follows from one or more manufacturing source to the final customers/end users either directly or through one or more levels like warehouses, distribution networks, distributors, etc.; bills of distribution are also known as the distribution network structure.

Marketing channel – The particular routing followed by an individual product or product shipment to its final destination (the end user or final customer); there are an endless number of possible marketing channels, which are made up of some combination of direct delivery, central warehouses, regional distribution centers, distribution centers, and retailers.

International Distribution Terms

Exporting – An international distribution strategy in which a company continues producing in their current mode and ships the goods abroad to international customers, either because the company was approached by a foreign customer, the company actively sought foreign customers, or the company sells to a middleman in the foreign country.

Licensing – An international distribution strategy in which a home company certifies a local company in another country to manufacture their product under their name with their expertise, support, and advice in return for payment; licensing saves the home company the cost of international shipping and operations while still making some profit off international markets.

Joint ventures – An international distribution strategy in which a home company joins forces with a local company in another country to produce the home company's product there; the home company invests capital and management; joint ventures give the home company the advantage of using an existing manufacturing and distribution system instead of building one.

Direct ownership – An international distribution strategy in which the home company develops or buys a completely new manufacturing and distribution system in another country; the home company assumes maximum risk and cost in comparison to other international distribution strategies, but also maximizes their profits and control.

Distribution channel – The means whereby products are physically moved from the manufacturing site to the end user.

Direct shipment – A distribution channel in which product is packaged at the manufacturer or distributor and then transported directly to the final customer; direct shipment is most efficient in cases where the volume shipped to the customer constitutes an entire container or delivery unit.

Consolidation shipment – A distribution channel in which a shipping agent combines shipments from multiple companies to constitute an entire container or delivery unit for transport to another country, where the container is unpacked and contents are dispersed to the individual recipients; consolidation shipment is most efficient when a company's shipments do not constitute an entire container or delivery unit.

Local distribution – A distribution channel in which company shipments are consolidated and transported in bulk to a foreign country and then dispersed through a distribution network to the individual customers; local distribution is most efficient when a company has many customers in the foreign country in question.

Intermodel transport - the utilization of two or more modes of transport in shipping goods from the manufacturer to their final destination. In international distribution, intermodel transport typically involves land transport by rail or road to an airport for air transport or to a port for sea transport to a foreign airport or port. From the foreign airport or port, the goods are once again transported over land by rail or road to the final customers, perhaps through an intermediate distributor. In some cases, as in North America, international distribution can be accomplished solely over land.

ATP

When the available-to-promise (ATP) quantity is non-cumulative, it is calculated and recorded for the first time period and subsequent time periods with MPS orders scheduled, without relationship to the ATP quantity for other periods. It is the ATP quantity for the time window in question, without regard to surplus ATP quantities from other time periods. The calculated ATP quantity is valid for the time period for which it is calculated and the subsequent time periods without MPS orders scheduled. In the first period, prior to scheduled MPS orders, it is calculated simply as the difference between the balance on hand and the total customer orders received to be filled before the next period in which a master production schedule (MPS) order is planned. The formula reads as follows: ATP = balance on hand – sum of customer orders received to be filled before the next time period in which an MPS order is scheduled.

For time periods after the opening time period with scheduled MPS orders, the ATP is calculated as the difference between the MPS-scheduled quantity to be produced and the sum of the customer orders received to be filled for the time period the MPS order is scheduled and the subsequent time periods until another MPS order is planned. The formula reads as follows: ATP = MPS order quantity – sum of customer orders received to be filled before the next time period in which an MPS order is scheduled.

As the name implies, the cumulative available-to-promise (ATP) quantity includes not only the ATP quantity specific to the given time segment for which it is computed but also the ATP quantities calculated for the previous time segments. The cumulative ATP quantity is calculated by determining the non-cumulative ATP for the time period in question and adding it to the ATP quantity calculated for the previous time segment, so each ATP quantity includes all ATP quantities that have gone before it. As with the non-cumulative ATP, the cumulative ATP is valid for the time period for which it is calculated and the subsequent time periods until an MPS order is scheduled, at which point it must be calculated again.

As customer orders are received, the total orders for the time period in question increase and the available-to-promise (ATP) quantity for the time period decreases. When the customer orders received for a period reach or exceed the initial ATP quantity for that period, the ATP quantity is zero. When this happens, it means that not enough product from that time period is available to fill customer orders. If the ATP quantity was non-cumulative, then ATP balances from previous time periods can be used to meet the demand. If the ATP quantity was cumulative, then product from the current and past periods is unavailable to meet customer orders and another means must be found. Two alternatives for handling this situation are partial deliveries and negotiated delivery dates. The manufacturer can offer to deliver the number of products available, a partial delivery, at the date originally requested. The second option is to offer a full delivery at a later date, in a manufacturing time period with a sufficient ATP quantity.

When a multi-level master production schedule (MPS) is in use, there is more than one source of demand for manufacturing components. For example, a component of the final product may also be sold as a spare part. In this case, the independent demand for the final product drives a dependent demand for the component while there is also an independent demand for the component as a spare part. It is necessary to keep track of and reconcile both demands simultaneously, so that the available-to-promise (ATP) quantity of components reflects only those components that are truly ATP, and not components to be used in higher levels of manufacturing. Similarly, the ATP end items must reflect only end items built with components earmarked for higher-level manufacturing and not those intended for sale as spare parts. The solution is to enter the dependent demand for component parts in higher-level manufacturing as customer orders on the component MPS.

FAS

When a final assembly schedule (FAS) is used for product customization, modules and major assemblies are usually master-scheduled. FAS planning is performed using the planning bill percentages of options sold to reserve material and capacity, and final assembly occurs in response to actual customer orders received. In this situation, the ATP facility needs to extend beyond the master schedule, so that customized goods can be promised realistically to customers. The ATP quantities of options available must reflect not only the master schedule, but also the planning bill percentages. The total ATP quantity cannot exceed the production scheduled in the master schedule, and the ATP quantities of the individual options cannot exceed the percentage breakdown of the total for those options specified in the planning bill.

Trading Groups

Three trading groups have emerged on the international scene: North America, Europe, and the Pacific Rim. The North American group was formed by the North American Free Trade Agreement (NAFTA) and consists of Canada, the United States, and Mexico. The European Union is the world's largest individual market, and contains most European nations. The Pacific Rim is formally named the Asia-Pacific Economic Cooperation and includes most nations with coastline on the Pacific Ocean. The European and North American blocks are considered more powerful, but the Pacific Rim block is expected to surpass the European market as the largest market in the near future. Competing effectively in the international market requires third-party verification such as certification and world-class status.

Governmental Requirements

Governments often apply laws and stipulations to the import and export of goods from their countries, and these laws and stipulations often differ significantly from those of a company's home country. When governments agree to buy international goods, or authorize internal businesses or individuals to buy international goods, they may in turn require investment in their country on the part of the exporting manufacturer or its country, the use of the country's own delivery infrastructure and companies, or counter trade. Counter trade allows both countries to increase their exports simultaneously rather than increasing one country's exports at the other country's expense.

TRANSPORTATION METHODS

The primary and interrelated considerations in a company's selection of its transportation methods are internal vs. external distribution, the mode of transport utilized, whether to use a distribution network, and the volume of goods being shipped. The size and nature of the industry and company in question play a large role in each of these considerations. In some situations, internal distribution is practically necessary, while in others it is more feasible to employ an outside specialist. In choosing a mode of delivery transport, air, road, rail, or sea, the weight- or volume-to-value ratio is the deciding factor. High-value, low-weight items are shipped through more expensive means, while low-value, high-weight items are shipped through less expensive means. Distribution networks give the advantage of combining modes of transport, and the different segments can be handled internally or externally individually. Finally, the volume of goods per shipment must be considered. Full loads are less expensive, but may not be feasible given the required delivery frequency.

IN TRANSIT OWNERSHIP

In transit inventory is goods that are in the process of being shipped between two or more geographic locations. In most cases, the goods remain the property of the party shipping the goods until the recipient accepts the delivery, at which point ownership is transferred. This includes manufacturing supplies delivered to a manufacturer by their supplier and finished goods delivered by the manufacturer to a distribution center or a customer. If a third party handles the delivery, the goods still remain in the possession of the sending company until the delivery is accepted. The primary exception to this procedure is in the case of international deliveries, when ownership of the goods often transfers before leaving the supplier's country through methods such as sight drafts and "free on board" shipping, as specified by the shipment terms.

TRANSPORTATION TERMS

Truckload lot (TL) – A freight term referring to a batch of goods to be shipped that constitutes an entire truckload, container, or other delivery unit; whether a shipment is a TL affects the price charged.

Less-than-truckload lot (LT) – A freight term referring to a batch of goods to be shipped that constitutes a partial or less than complete truckload, container, or other delivery unit; whether a shipment is a TL or LT affects the price charged.

Load leveling – The practice of leveling work or distribution load evenly over time so that the work or distribution load density is constant rather than variable; since distribution is driven by demand which is often variable and time-dependent, distribution load leveling can be challenging; one solution is to use external distribution exclusively, or to maintain a consistent level of internal distribution and supplement with external distribution as necessary.

IMPORTANT TERMS

Demand management – The overarching process of identifying, orchestrating, and fulfilling the market requirement for goods and services, including predicting demand, filling orders, serving customers, and planning distribution.

Planning hierarchy – The multi-level interdependent structure of general and specific business planning beginning with the mission statement, supported by the corporate and business strategies, which in turn are under girded by the four functional strategies for marketing, finance, engineering, and manufacturing.

Mission statement – A succinct presentation of a company's goals and general methods for reaching those goals and the corresponding results to be achieved; a mission statement must be well balanced so that clear direction is given without limiting the company's future scope.

Corporate strategy – An overall plan for the company based on the mission statement, but with specific rather than general goals; the corporate strategy includes the business strategy.

Business strategy – A segment of the top-level corporate strategy setting forth the direction of the business; the business strategy should draw from the organization's strengths in order to maximize its competitiveness.

Marketing strategy – A functional plan developed from and supporting the corporate and business strategies defining a company's target market segment, identifying a company's market niche, and evaluating the competition.

Financial strategy – A functional plan developed from and supporting the corporate and business strategies detailing the generation of financial resources (investment strategy) and management of those resources to meet obligations and goals.

Engineering strategy – A functional plan developed from and supporting the corporate and business strategies detailing the framework for designing and developing new products and their corresponding manufacturing processes and supplying the specialized, multi-disciplinary skill sets necessary for both; the engineering strategy can also be called the product development strategy.

Manufacturing strategy – A functional plan developed from and supporting the corporate and business strategies setting forth guidelines for building manufacturing capabilities and infrastructure to fulfill the organizational goals; the manufacturing strategy is often overlooked, and can also be called the operations strategy.

Customer service – a company's ability to respond effectively to their customers' needs, questions, and requests as well as to deliver the requested product at the customer's preferred time.

Customer service ratio – a customer service performance measurement calculating the percentage of orders, order line items, or order dollar values that are delivered accurately and on time.

Performance standard – the targeted goal for a particular performance measurement

Priority rules – Standards in place in a company for the sequence in which customer orders will be handled; this is especially important in situations where manufacturing supplies or end items are in short supply or materials move very quickly; some examples of priority rules include first-come, first-serve, handling designated key customers first, and handling in order of profitability.

Customer service level – the standard or target goal for customer service set as company policy by high level management; the customer service level must be set by high level management because of the high cost incurred from the safety stock and distribution level necessary to maintain it.

Delivery performance –a measurement of customer service effectiveness, particularly in the area of distribution, focusing on deliveries made to customers, including percentage of on-time deliveries, the customer service ratio, the longest delivery time, the delivery time variability, and the average order-processing lead time.

Standard containers – reusable bins, cartons, or boxes, all of uniform size and with separators, which serves as the primary container for material handling; the separators eliminate the need for counting individual items since a quick check verifies the number of items, simplifying delivery and customer service.

Responsiveness-is the ability and willingness of a company to meet their customer's needs and requests, often a function of the company's lead time. Increasing responsiveness requires decreasing lead-time, which can be accomplished through several means. Streamlining the customer order and order entry process, providing automated ordering, decreasing manufacturing lead time, and master scheduling modules and subassemblies to shorten lead times for customized goods are all viable lead time reducers. Some responsiveness performance measurements include average order processing time, manufacturing lead time, percentage of on-time deliveries, and order processing lead-time variability.

Safety stock-is the material that a company keeps in inventory at all times in order to protect themselves against fluctuations in the supply of materials for production or goods available for sale and errors in demand forecasting. More specifically, safety stock acts as a buffer against variability in demand over time, provides goods during stock replenishment time, and maintains the customer service level at all points during the manufacturing cycle. Extensive safety stock is especially important in industries and companies with long lead times for stock replenishment. In short, the purpose of safety stock is for a company to be able to provide goods to customers at all times, regardless of current circumstances, but this purpose must be balanced with the high cost of maintaining safety stock.

Safety stock calculation - can be calculated statistically according to the following formula: safety stock = (standard deviation) * (safety factor) * (Sqrt [lead time/forecast time period]), where the standard deviation is of the demand experienced over time and the safety factor is determined by the desired customer service level. The standard deviation can be approximated using the formula standard deviation = 1.25 * (mean average deviation). The desired customer service level is set by management, and then looked up in the table of safety factors for the normal distribution to determine the corresponding safety factor (in number of standard deviations).

Developing and Validating the Master Schedule

Master Scheduling

Master scheduling is the process of transforming high-level, aggregate plans (the production plan) into practical schedules for execution by suppliers and manufacturing. Through master scheduling, various aspects of manufacturing come together and specific goals are communicated throughout the organization. The master schedule is consistent with both the upper level production plan and the lower level master production schedule (MPS) and is informed by production and capacity resource availability, internal and external supply and demand information, planning bills, resource bills, customer orders, and demand forecasts. The master schedule is developed from the production plan, and from it is developed the MPS, which is verified for feasibility using rough-cut capacity planning.

Purpose

Through master scheduling, production is orchestrated to provide a balanced workload to manufacturing, to produce goods economically, to support the sales plan, and to meet customer demands for product. Specifically, these objectives are met through providing a schedule for manufacturing, stocking in preparation for final assembly if a final assembly schedule is used, providing input to material requirements planning (MRP) and rough-cut capacity planning (RCCP), and establishing a basis for committing to customer orders. It is through master scheduling that all manufacturing factors are tied together, linking the shipment of goods to customers all the way back to materials management.

Master Scheduler

The primary function of the master scheduler is the development and maintenance of the master schedule. The master schedule is developed from the production plan and must meet the needs of all departments and demands within the company, including marketing, finance, manufacturing, planning, purchasing, distribution, customer needs, required delivery dates, shop capacities, and more. The pre-sales and operations planning meeting is often chaired by the master scheduler, providing input from the master scheduler to the actual sales and operations planning meeting. The master scheduler is often referred to as the anchorman due to the central, coordinating function required from this role. A successful master scheduler needs to be an innovator and a good communicator who is positive and experienced in manufacturing, sales and marketing, planning, and inventory.

Senior Executives

Senior management, usually the CEO and those who report directly to the CEO, are responsible for top level planning. In the sales and operations planning process they produce the sales and production plans which should guide the workings of the company to fulfill the company's strategic plan. The production plan is the basis for the master schedule. Ideally, creating and maintaining the production plan should be the extent of senior management's role in managing the master schedule, but this is not always or even usually the case since problems can arise in developing a master schedule from the production plan. If there are problems, the master scheduler must consult senior management to arrive at a feasible solution that still meets company objectives. The solution may involve changes to the production plan.

Top Management Planning

In top management planning, the business plan, sales and marketing forecast, and resource availability per time period are used by high-level executives to develop the company's plan for the future, specifically the sales plan and the production plan. The sales plan specifies the planned sales for future periods by family groups. This information is used to set specific regional, area, and individual sales targets. The production plan corresponds to the sales plan and sets the product quantities to be manufactured in future periods by family group. This information is then used in the master scheduling process to develop the master production schedule (MPS), which sets the specific manufacturing schedule to achieve the company's goals. In short, top management planning produces, among other things, the production plan, which is the primary input to the master scheduling process.

Schedule

The master scheduler receives the approved sales and production plans generated by company executives in the monthly sales and operations planning meeting. The master scheduler must then convert the production plan, usually in quantities to be manufactured per product family per month, into a master schedule and master production schedule (MPS), usually in quantity to be manufactured per product per week. This is done on a monthly basis. Every month, the master scheduler takes an additional month's requirements from the production plan and translates it to the MPS. At this time, the master scheduler also incorporates any changes to the production plan approved in the sales and operations meeting into the MPS. The production quantities shown on the production plan and the MPS must line up. In the same way, the sales plan is translated into forecast demand quantities on the master schedule.

Schedule Stabilization

For the master schedule to be effective, it must be stable. Changes made to the master schedule should, first of all, be minimized. Beyond that, changes that are found to be essential must be made with due consideration to their effect on the master schedule itself as well as the lower levels of planning. If too many changes are made to the master schedule the changes become unmanageable, resulting in material shortages and required start and finish dates in the past. As this occurs, manufacturing will ignore the schedule since it is untenable, leading to a loss of manufacturing control. Some tools that can be used to stabilize the master schedule are master scheduling rules, hedging, options over-planning, safety stock, safety capacity, and safety lead time.

Schedule Guidelines

Some general guidelines for maintaining an effective master schedule include the following: a stable lower level schedule must be maintained for effective manufacturing control, which is accomplished through commitment to the stability of the master schedule itself; agreement on and commitment to time fences, including a frozen period, is crucial in controlling the master schedule to keep it practical and feasible; the fact of necessary changes must be accepted, but these changes must be made with regard to material and capacity availability and make appropriate trade-offs rather than trying to maintain an unfeasible number of objectives; inaccurate forecasting must be dealt with through improving the forecasting process and/or buffering for inaccuracies through means such as safety stock or offsetting MPS time requirements; and the master scheduler must not over-commit resources or capacity when developing the master production schedule (MPS).

Schedule Flexibility

Keeping the master schedule flexible does not imply that continual changes are acceptable, but rather that changes deemed essential can be made with appropriate consideration to their feasibility. One method for increasing flexibility is utilizing a final assembly schedule (FAS), in which case modules and subassemblies are master scheduled and end products are assembled according to a FAS in response to customer orders. Another approach to the FAS technique is scheduling final assembly to maintain equal run-out quantities of end items in finished goods inventory rather than scheduling in response to customer orders. Another method for increasing flexibility is master scheduling typicals, in which case the average material and capacity requirements for a product family are master scheduled but manufacturing occurs only in response to customer orders. When using typicals, the product ordered by a customer to be manufactured replaces a typical in the master schedule.

Appropriate Tools

Since the master scheduling function is critical to the success of the company, it is important to provide the appropriate tools for the master scheduler to work with, particularly in the area of software. The right tools boost the efficiency and effectiveness of the master scheduling process. The applications of knowledge-based decision support systems such as making and testing trial master production schedules (MPS's), performing rough-cut capacity planning, capacity planning, balancing workload, a detailed available-to-promise (ATP) facility, and more specific tools applicable to the industry and environment in question all aid the master scheduling process. Although these functions can usually be performed manually, the computing power of computer systems substantially increases the speed and frequency with which these calculations can be performed and compared.

Relationship to Manufacturing Modules

The elements or modules of a manufacturing system are highly interrelated and interdependent. Sales and operations planning include demand forecasting, development of the sales and production plans, and resource planning. The order entry process captures the actual demand for product. Sales and operations planning and order entry together serve as inputs to the master scheduling process. The master scheduling process itself includes development of the master production schedule (MPS), rough-cut capacity planning, and final assembly scheduling. Master scheduling in turn serves as input to the detailed scheduling and planning process, which includes both material requirements planning (MRP) and capacity requirements planning (CRP).

Operations Management Planning

Operations management planning revolves around disaggregating the production plan into the individual end items required per time period and determining and setting into motion the actions required to fulfill the plan. The production plan, the sales forecast, the available inventory, and the item master file planning data are all inputs to the operations management planning process. In essence, operations management planning entails master scheduling and it's supporting functions. The supporting functions include rough-cut capacity planning, to verify the feasibility of the schedule, and distribution requirements planning (DRP), to verify that demand will be met on schedule. The master production schedule (MPS), part of the output of master scheduling, feeds material requirements planning (MRP), which is in turn supported by capacity requirements planning (CRP), to verify that the material plan is feasible, and planning data, to inform the process.

Manufacturing Management

The master schedule is the manufacturing plan, and as such is a critical element in manufacturing management. Two items that are inexorably linked to the feasibility and success of the master schedule are capacity and materials. The master schedule is verified by rough-cut capacity planning, but, as the name implies, this process is general and not specific. Once material requirements planning (MRP) is performed using the master production schedule (MPS), the material plan is verified using capacity requirements planning (CRP). CRP is more exact than rough-cut capacity planning, and the result may indicate that careful load balancing is required to meet the material plan. If the prescribed load cannot be balanced across the available capacity, the master scheduling process must be revisited. It is clear that master scheduling feeds into both materials and capacity management, and at the same time materials and capacity management feed back into master scheduling when necessary.

MANUFACTURING ENVIRONMENT

The master scheduling process is always linked to the production plan, but how the two are linked depends on the manufacturing environment in question. More specifically, the level of the product structure that is master scheduled is dependent on the manufacturing environment. In general, standard bills of material are used to master schedule standard products, while planning bills are used to master schedule non-standard products. When a limited number of product configurations are offered for sale, then the module level is master scheduled and a final assembly schedule based on planning bills is used to build the final configurations to replenish the warehouse. When true customization of products is offered through options and choices, manufacture of subassemblies and material flow are master scheduled and final products are built using a final assembly schedule based on actual customer orders. Planning bills and standard bills are used to plan material supplies in preparation for final assembly.

SUPER BILL

The production plan specifies the quantity to be produced per family group per time period. In order to convert this information into a practical master production schedule (MPS) specifying the quantity per item to be produced, decisions have to be made regarding the product spread within the family to be produced. Although the forecast quantity changes over time, it is assumed that the spread within the family is always similar. The super bill specifies the percentage of individual products within the family that make up the total family sales based on past history. This percentage is then applied to the production plan family quantity to determine the quantities of the individual items within the family to be produced.

Through production planning, the number of customizable items to be produced is specified, but the options or customizations are not. In order to plan materials and production, decisions have to be made regarding the customizations to be produced. For this purpose, a super bill is kept that specifies the percentages of specific customizations that make up total sales. It is assumed that although the demand quantity changes, the spread of options sold remains similar. Planners then apply the percentages from the super bill to the production quantity to determine the number of each customization to plan for. These numbers are used to plan and provide the material supply for production and master scheduling modules. The final customized products are built according to a final assembly schedule once customer orders are received.

TYPICALS

Master scheduling with typicals is a technique for planning production when precise demand quantities within a product family cannot be determined. Average amounts of materials and labor required to produce products within the family determine typicals, which are then used as the planning unit. Material and capacity are master scheduled based on these typicals, rather than on actual requirements for individual items within the product family. Products are not actually manufactured until customer orders are received, but master scheduling the material and capacity allows manufacturing to proceed once the order is received rather than waiting for material and capacity availability, shortening the lead time experienced by the customer.

Marketing and Sales Performance

Marketing and sales performance measures include not only evaluation of the sales and production plans for effectiveness, which measures the performance of the sales and operations planning function, but also the determination of the company's overall success in meeting customer demand, even when that demand varies from anticipated demand. Although overlapping, the two are not identical. Some specific marketing and sales performance measures include the percentage of master production schedule (MPS) manufacturing orders completed on time, the percentages of final assembly schedule (FAS) units completed on time, the percentage of MPS items changed within the demand and planning time fences, the fulfillment rate of customer promises based on the available-to-promise (ATP) facility, and the overall fulfillment rate of customer promises.

Purchasing

Purchasing is the process of finding and contracting with suppliers to provide materials for manufacturing. Purchasing is a critical component of successfully executing the master schedule. Material quality, on time delivery, and accuracy of standard lead times are the factors by which purchasing performance is judged. Supplier quality is determined by counting the number and/or calculating the percentage of good or faulty items received, until a supplier has established their quality to the point that checking is no longer necessary. The number and/or percentage of deliveries made on time is/are tracked to gauge on time delivery. This performance measure is especially important when deliveries are made to the point of use as they are needed. Delays can cause unplanned production downtime. The accuracy of standard lead times on file is also the responsibility of the purchasing function and is important because this data is used in master schedule and master production schedule (MPS) calculations. If the standard lead times are incorrect, then the schedules are based on faulty information.

Unrealistic Master Schedule Consequences

The consequences of an unrealistic master schedule are severe since the master schedule drives the production process, ensuring the availability of products to meet commitments made to customers. When the master schedule is unrealistic, work centers become overloaded, customer service is poor, and priority systems are meaningless. Overloaded work centers can be due to general overloading that occurs as a result of over committing materials and/or capacity on the master production schedule (MPS), front end loading caused by material shortages or halted production, or an incomplete master schedule. Poor customer service is failure to meet obligations to customers, and can be the result of unstable MPS's, insufficient planning horizons, or thoughtless and unrealistic commitments made to customers. Meaningless priority systems result when manufacturing is extremely overloaded, but urgent work is simply moved to the front of the queue and the overall situation remains the same.

Invalid Master Schedule

An invalid master schedule is one that is imbalanced or unrealistic. This can occur due to improper master scheduling or too many schedule changes made to an acceptable master schedule. If the schedule was invalid to begin with, then the problem is in the master scheduling process itself. Rough-cut capacity planning (RCCP) and level scheduling should be considered when this is the case. Subsequent changes to the master schedule can be caused by changed customer requirements, changed demand forecasts due to economic changes or other marketing revisions, and manufacturing back-ups caused by material supply problems or other issues. Some other common causes of invalid master schedules include front-end loading, rush orders, cancellations, and inaccurate records.

CUSTOMER CHANGES

After initially placing an order, customers may request changes to the order delivery date, contents, or design. These changes can be costly to the manufacturer, depending on how far the processing has progressed when the change is requested and the magnitude of the change. Delaying the delivery date is generally easy to handle, but scrapping a complete or almost complete production batch in favor of a new design is costly, especially if an alternate use cannot be found for the goods. Manufacturers must each develop their own policy for these situations, whether to accept changes, what changes to accept, and whether to absorb the cost internally or pass it on to the customer. The nature of the relationship with the customer in question is an important consideration. Whatever is decided, the master schedule must be changed and re-balanced accordingly.

RUSH ORDERS

Rush orders are orders that must be completed in less time than the normal lead time, either because the customer ordered the goods for a quick delivery date or for some other reason. To complete the order on time, a priority system of some sort must be used. Suppliers may have to be enlisted to provide materials more quickly than usual, and internally the order is processed ahead of the regularly scheduled production, possibly causing subsequent delays. Obviously there is a cost associated with rush orders, and each manufacturer must develop a suitable policy for their situation, whether to accept rush orders, in what conditions to accept rush orders, and whether to absorb the cost internally or pass it on to the customer. As always, the nature of the manufacturer's relationship with the customer in question is an important consideration. Whatever is decided, the master schedule must be changed and re-balanced accordingly.

CANCELLATIONS

When customers cancel orders, the order processing is stopped immediately. Costs incurred due to cancellations include materials ordered for the job that cannot be returned or used elsewhere and the processing that has already occurred. If the order has not begun processing, then there is no problem. When a completed or nearly completed large specialty order is cancelled, the cost can be very high. A cancellation fee can be charged to the canceling customer based on the expensed incurred by the manufacturer due to the cancellation. The order must also be deleted from the master schedule, freeing up capacity and materials.

DOWNTIME

Unplanned downtime typically causes production delays and ultimately unmet deadlines. If manufacturing cannot catch back up with the master schedule after the downtime has ended, then rescheduling is required. Even when the downtime is planned, it can be difficult to handle if a manufacturing facility typically runs at complete utilization. Handling equipment downtime is even more difficult when the machine in question is a bottleneck workstation. In this case, downtime is usually translated directly into completion delays. Two solutions for preventing and handling downtime are preventive maintenance of equipment and running operations under capacity. Through preventive maintenance, machinery is cleaned, adjusted, and replaced at appropriate intervals to prevent breakdowns. The preventive maintenance sessions must be scheduled along with manufacturing. Running operations below capacity increases flexibility so that downtime is easier to handle.

INACCURATE RECORDS

Manufacturing planning and control relies heavily on information. This information is stored in records that are accessed as needed. For the system to be effective, the records must be accurate. If the records are incorrect, the resulting calculations informing the master schedule and the master schedule itself will also be incorrect. Bills of material, routings, purchasing records, and inventory records are some of the information on which the master schedule depends. Standard minimum accuracy requirements are 99% for bills of material and routings and 95% for purchasing and inventory records. The levels of accuracy must be monitored and sources of inaccuracies identified and resolved. It is a continuous process with a goal of 100% accuracy.

Batch

Batch manufacturing is a manufacturing process in which lots or groups of goods are produced repeatedly, usually regularly according to demand. Standard bills of material and product routings are employed. Either standard end items or modules for configured end items can be master scheduled.

Project

Project manufacturing is a manufacturing process entailing the design, construction, and possibly installation of highly specialized, one-time, major products. As is the case with engineer-to-order production environments, the project manufacturing process is difficult to master schedule and application of master scheduling is highly specific to the industry, environment, and situation. Once the design is finalized, bills of material may be created for use in planning. From there, the major segments and sub-assemblies may be master scheduled.

Remanufacturing/Rebuilding

In remanufacturing/rebuilding manufacturing processes, normal master scheduling is not feasible since the work content is not established until the item is in the plant being worked on. Instead, average times and bills of material for the products that are rebuilt can be used to master schedule material and capacity.

Repairing/Overhauling

In repairing and overhauling manufacturing processes, time, materials, and cost required cannot be established until the item is examined. Regularly used parts can be maintained in stock using a replenishment system, and master scheduling is used to reserve time and plan future loading.

Process

In process manufacturing there is considerable variety. When standard items are produced through continuous or batch manufacturing, master scheduling is the same as in make-to-stock production environments. The end items themselves or product families are master scheduled. When product families are master scheduled, planning bills are used. If products are made to order, end items are master scheduled once orders are received and future planning is performed through the use of typicals to ensure material and capacity availability.

Two-Level Master

When master scheduling of a product family occurs in conjunction with a planning bill or family bill for that product family, it is called two-level master production scheduling. In this situation, master scheduling occurs on two levels: the overall product family planning which is included on the master schedule itself and the breakdown of product family planning for the individual products using the associated planning bill percentage spreads. Thus the planning is handled simultaneously on two levels, the product family as a whole and the individual items one level down.

Multi-Level Master

When demand for goods is felt on more than one level of manufacturing, the finished product and some component of the finished product, for example, it is called multi-level master scheduling. The master schedule must accommodate both the demand for the end item and the demand for the component. The demand for the component consists of two elements, the dependent demand derived from the independent demand for end items and the independent demand for the component itself. This situation can occur when a company manufactures an item and replacement parts for the item or supplies more than one company with components in various stages. The master schedule must account for multiple sets of requirements from independent and dependent sources on different levels of manufacturing.

Formulating the Master Production Schedule

Both the original development and the ongoing maintenance of the master production schedule (MPS) involve four steps. The first step is to identify the sources of requirements. These product demands can originate in customer orders that have been received, finished goods warehouses that need to be stocked, demand for spare parts for manufactured products, maintenance of safety stock levels, orders received from other plants (interplant orders), and forecast demands. The second step in developing the MPS is establishing the schedule of factory requirements, which differ from the requirement sources. The requirements from the original sources must be quantified and translated into a practical production plan, with consideration given to the current stock levels, the batch sizes produced, and manufacturing capacity limitations. The third step is the actual creation of the MPS, which is a trial-and-error process until a feasible schedule that meets all requirements is generated. The final stage in formulating the MPS is the implementation.

Schedule Changes

The first consideration in making changes to the master production schedule (MPS) is whether the changes are really necessary and whether they are worth the cost incurred. All orders are not good orders when it comes to the company's well being. When changes are deemed essential, the first step is to determine the necessity of the previously planned manufacturing. There may be non-essential production included in the original plan that can be deleted. If production orders were delayed due to the change, the market for those goods may already be lost, especially in off-the-shelf businesses, so those jobs can be deleted without further penalty. If deleting jobs is not an option or if the schedule is still overloaded after jobs are deleted, rescheduling work in the future is the best solution. Manufacturing can consult with marketing about which jobs would be best rescheduled for a later date or a new manufacturing priority list, and manufacturing planning and execution can proceed accordingly.

General Overloading

General overloading occurs when too much work is planned on the master production schedule (MPS). In this situation, the planned work will not be completed. Shortages will be experienced at the higher-level assemblies, and finished products will be overdue. If general overloading is consistently the case, there is no room for rescheduling jobs even thought the existing MPS is untenable. A major reschedule will be in order, with all of the associated difficulties and problems.

Front End Loading

Front end loading occurs not because the original MPS was unrealistic, but because progress is halted at some point due to a material shortage or other production problem. Although the cause is different, the result is similar to the result in general overloading, except that there is not an ongoing problem but rather a quantity of extra work to be performed. The backup incurred can be resolved through subcontracting, working extra hours or shifts, delaying the production if the goods are not immediately necessary, or canceling the production if feasible.

Poor Customer Service

Poor customer service occurs when customers are dissatisfied with the service provided, due to ineffective company policies resulting in lost business. Two similar causes of poor customer service are unstable master production schedules (MPS's) and short MPS time horizons. An unstable master production schedule (MPS) results when a company does not adhere to the MPS time fence policies. A short MPS time horizon occurs when the time horizon is less than the required lead time. In both cases material and capacity shortages result since sufficient lead time is not available to meet the need once the need is established and ultimately resulting in missed production deadlines and poor customer service. When sales and/or marketing personnel make thoughtless, unrealistic promises to customers, poor customer service also results. The order promise date can be missed altogether, or it can be prioritized and met at the cost of other order deadlines. Either way, poor customer service results.

Sources for Master Production Scheduling

Bills of material define the goods necessary for manufacturing, as well as provide associated costing information. Routings establish the operations and the capacity of each necessary for manufacturing. Bills of labor and resources identify the amount and type of personnel skills and resources required. Common parts bills and percentage bills are planning bills specifying the breakdown of options required within a customizable product. All of these records are specific to the part being manufactured and are the basis of operations planning calculations. If they are incorrect, then the master production schedule (MPS) will be incorrect as well. All should be monitored regularly to aid maintenance of the 99% accuracy required.

Demand Forecast

When the demand forecast included in the master production schedule (MPS) is incorrect, the actual orders received do not line up with the planned orders. Since the demand forecast is used to plan for the effect of future sales on available stock, the projected available stock balances will be incorrect. When the projected available stock balances are incorrect, future planning is based on erroneous data and thus shortages or surpluses can occur.

Actual Customer Demand

When the actual customer demand, or the customer orders received, in the MPS is incorrect, the actual customer demand and the figure used for actual customer demand in the MPS do not correlate, and the resulting MPS calculations are incorrect. The actual customer demand is used to calculate the quantity of goods available to promise to customers, so mistakes result in faulty customer commitments. Either customer orders are denied unnecessarily or untenable commitments are made resulting in missed deliveries.

Stock on Hand

When the stock on hand included in the master production schedule (MPS) is incorrect, either stock is in inventory but not used since it is not recorded properly, or stock is assumed to be in inventory that is not. This number is also used in calculating the projected available balances and the available to promise (ATP) quantities. MPS orders are also used in calculating the projected available balances and ATP quantities, so faulty MPS order data result in faulty projected available balances and ATP quantities. When the projected available stock balances are incorrect, future planning is based on erroneous data and thus shortages or surpluses can occur. Since the ATP quantities are the basis for making promises to customers, incorrect ATP quantities lead to unnecessary denials to customer orders or untenable customer commitments and ultimately missed deliveries.

ENGINEERING CHANGE CONTROL

Engineering change control is a technique for managing engineering changes. In engineering change control, anyone within the company or even a customer can submit engineering change requests with supporting documentation to an engineering change order board. The board consists of all department managers and is chaired by a high-level company executive. All members of the board receive the change requests in advance and consider them with respect to their own department prior to meeting together. The board meets to engage in informed discussion of the change requests and makes a joint decision regarding the change. An engineering change controller serves as the administrator of the process, receiving and distributing change requests, communicating board decisions to change requestors, and disseminating engineering change orders appropriately.

Engineering changes are implemented by updating the appropriate bills of material to reflect the changes. Since bills of material are the roadmap for manufacturing, their contents should be tightly controlled. Personnel responsible for making approved changes to the bills of material must have access to the bills of material contents, but it should be a small group of people with no connection to production or material handling. It is preferable that bill of material change staff be part of the quality or standards department. Free access to read the bills of material must be readily available, but free access to change bills of material leads to problems. When engineering changes would affect the current master production schedule (MPS), they must be planned and implemented in conjunction with the master scheduler and marketing.

CHANGE NOTIFICATION

When a proposed engineering change is officially accepted, an engineering change note or engineering change order is formulated and distributed to all concerned staff and departments within the company, including the planner. The planner then relates the engineering change to the affected suppliers directly or through other means of communication established in the supplier partnership. The supplier uses the information to purchase the correct raw materials and produce parts that line up with the change. Ideally, the supplier should be aware of proposed changes before they are approved and implemented so that the supplier is prepared for the change. Timely communication with the supplier regarding changes is essential to avoid obsolete inventory at every stage and to insure that the supplier meets customer requirements so that the customer's manufacturing is not interrupted.

SUPPLIER CHANGES

In long-term supplier relationships, which are the ideal, supplier changes usually occur as a result of the supplier's inability to provide the necessary performance level. New suppliers go through a thorough, multi-disciplinary assessment, possibly even supplier certification. If handled appropriately, such a change in suppliers does not interfere with master scheduling or manufacturing output.

Changes in supplies, either the materials not meeting specifications or not being delivered on time, can occur internally or externally. Internally, changes in supply quality or timeliness can be caused by material problems, quality issues, or machine breakdowns in the lower levels of manufacturing, ultimately resulting in rushed final assembly or missed order promise dates. Externally, changes in supply quality or timeliness are caused by similar problems, but under the supplier's control. Unacceptable quality levels or late deliveries in supplied materials can hamper manufacturing through delays. Good supplier communication is crucial in anticipating and resolving these problems.

An effective master production schedule (MPS) depends on the availability of manufacturing supplies when they are required, which hinges on good supplier relationships and up-to-date purchasing lead times in the material requirements planning (MRP) input data. When materials will not be available as planned, the master scheduler must intervene. The best option is to investigate alternative means to supply the material on time, such as using a different supplier, expediting shipping, reducing order quantity, or otherwise working with the supplier. If no way is found to provide material on time, then the master scheduler must consider alterations to the master schedule. This is done by determining the MPS items affected by the shortage and how to make the best possible use of available resources. What items should be manufactured first and which customer orders should be filled first must be determined in coordination with marketing and the customers. For customers who were ordering to stock inventory, a delay might not be problematic, but for those ordering direct to their manufacturing line a delay may be unacceptable.

Capacity Changes

The master production schedule (MPS) is dependent on material supply for execution. The material supply is dependent on capacity availability both internally in the lower levels of manufacturing and externally in supplier facilities to produce the required goods. Successful execution of the MPS thus depends on capacity. Ensuring an external supplier's future capacity availability is usually done through long-term supplier relationships and partnerships. Systems such as the release system and scheduling the vendor in conjunction with long-term contracts and agreements are means of communicating material requirements planning (MRP) and ensuring long-term capacity availability. It is increasingly common for companies to work with their suppliers to increase supplier capacity if necessary since finding alternative suppliers is so time-consuming. Internally, rough-cut capacity planning is used to verify the availability of the necessary capacity to meet the MPS. If the MPS does end up causing irresolvable requirement-capacity imbalances or overloading, the master scheduler can increase the capacity to meet the need or recommend reducing the planned production.

The three types of manufacturing capacities are labor, equipment, and tooling. Labor refers to the workers involved in manufacturing. The most important factor in considering labor as a manufacturing capacity is workforce flexibility. If the workers are cross-trained and can thus perform multiple functions, shifting workers around in overload situations can be an invaluable solution. Machinery is the equipment used in the manufacturing process. Machinery cannot generally be increased quickly, so adding equipment is a long-term rather than a short-term solution. If equipment in a manufacturing facility is utilized at its maximum capacity, increasing the amount of time the equipment is used through overtime or additional shifts could be a solution. The tooling refers to the fixtures that customize the equipment to specific manufacturing uses. Like the machinery, the tooling usually cannot be increased quickly. Increasing the amount of time the tooling is used through overtime and extra shifts could be a quick solution.

Alternatives to Resolve Insufficient Capacity

Alternate routings, order quantity alterations, worker overtime, additional shifts, work force repositioning, and subcontracting are all alternatives available to ease or resolve capacity insufficiencies. Alternate routings involve manufacturing product differently than usual in order to use equipment that is not overloaded. Decreasing the order quantities to the minimum required to satisfy immediate customer needs also reduces workload on overloaded equipment or work centers. Extra hours in the short-term and extra shifts in the long-term on the part of the workforce increase capacity. Repositioning the work force can resolve capacity limitations when the problem is due to insufficient labor available at a problem work center. This is only possible with a flexible workforce. Finally, subcontracting work from the bottleneck operations can ease the manufacturing burden. Subcontracting is only a short-term solution if there are established subcontractors due to the time involved in selecting and qualifying new subcontractors. Two or more of these techniques can also be used in combination.

Planned Capacity Changes

Reasons for planned capacity increases include easing the execution of the master schedule, especially in the case of overloaded work centers, and improving customer service by reducing lead time. Capacity can decrease due to insufficient resources, manufacturing rescheduling, rush jobs, and equipment malfunctions. Capacity changes can be temporary or permanent. Short-term capacity increases can be accomplished through sub-contracting, purchasing rather than manufacturing components or end items, repositioning flexible labor, allowing worker overtime, or adding shifts. Adding capital equipment and/or facilities is the strategy for permanent capacity increase. When capacity is decreased, which is usually unexpected, the master production schedule (MPS) must be changed so that production quantities can be met. One safeguard against negative effects of capacity changes is to reserve a set percentage of capacity as a buffer, which can then be used in case of unanticipated decreases.

Changes to Major Customer Orders

Major customers are those who place large, ongoing orders with a manufacturer. When these customers change their orders, it can be difficult for the manufacturer to handle, especially if the changes are unexpected increases. Unexpected decreases can cause financial problems since capacity and labor would be underutilized as a result. The primary way to prevent such difficulties is through good customer relationships marked by open communication. Supply methods such as the release system and vendor scheduling provide early, automatic communication of customer needs. It is in the best interest of the manufacturer to receive their customers' plans as early as possible so that manufacturing plans can be made accordingly. One safeguard against unanticipated changes to major customer orders is reserving safety capacity to deal with the unexpected. It is also a good business practice not to commit to customer requests without first verifying the company's ability to comply with those requests.

Design and Engineering Changes

The primary reasons behind design and/or engineering changes are resolving problems with the current design, improving the product, or handling the discontinuation of raw materials or component parts. The extent of the ramifications of the change depends on the level of urgency. If a safety-related design problem must be resolved, it is done immediately, even if it requires breaking into the frozen period. Changes that are less urgent in nature will be implemented with consideration given to current inventory, the logistics of tooling changes, and time phasing requirements. Manufacturing practices such as low inventory, quick changeovers, simplicity of design, and interdisciplinary and concurrent design make the change process easier. Frozen periods should not be disrupted, and changes should commence at the start of a new frozen period. These types of changes are handled through engineering change control.

Incomplete Master Schedules

Incomplete master schedules occur in companies that make standard as well as specialized products, but opt not to master schedule the specialized products. If capacity and material are not reserved for the production of specialized goods, then adding them in later can interfere with the scheduled work on standard items. In this situation, the scheduled work typically becomes overdue.

Priority Systems

Priority systems are mechanisms for speeding urgent production orders through manufacturing in order to meet a deadline that is off schedule or a special customer need. Rushing an order comes at a cost to the regularly scheduled production. Priority systems become meaningless when they are used as a solution to an overloading problem, and when de-expediting is not used in conjunction with expediting. Expediting is the process of prioritizing an order to process it through production ahead of scheduled orders. De-expediting is the process of removing that prioritization when it is no longer necessary or when a more important order comes along. If expediting is used excessively and de-expediting is not used, the result is a long queue of priority jobs trickling through manufacturing. Expediting sparingly and in conjunction with de-expediting minimizes the effect on scheduled manufacturing and keeps priority systems relevant by not overloading them.

Linear programming

Some examples of complex problems that can be solved through the use of linear programming in the master scheduling process include the planning of production for a seasonal demand market while minimizing costs associated with hiring, laying off, subcontracting, and holding inventory; the determination of production levels by plant and plant-warehouse supply relationships in a multiple plant, multiple warehouse organization; the determination of the most profitable mix of end items to be produced given specific constraints on material and capacity; and the scheduling of multiple products through one manufacturing work center while minimizing set-up and carrying costs, meeting demand, and not exceeding capacity.

Pegging

Pegging is helpful in manufacturing situations when supply problems such as material shortages and late deliveries arise. In dealing with the problem, the first step is to determine the scope of its effect. Pegging information is used for that purpose. Where in the planning the affected materials were to be used and the relationship of the affected materials to all levels of planned manufacturing can be determined through pegging. With this information, decisions can be made about how to proceed with manufacturing, specifically what can be done most effectively with the available resources. Single-level pegging identifies an item's parent part only, while full-level pegging identifies requirements all the way to the ultimate end item. Both can be used, but single-level pegging provides the information one step at a time rather than all at once in one record, as is the case with full-level pegging.

Bottom-up re-planning

Some techniques that can be used to perform bottom-up re-planning in the case of material shortages are batch size reduction, reduction of inter-operation time, and order or operation splitting. Batch size reduction is the decrease in quantity of the production lot size to the maximum number that can be produced with the material available, instead of putting the whole lot on hold until the shortage is resolved. Reduction of inter-operation time is reducing or eliminating queue times for a particular production lot to process it through manufacturing more quickly to resolve a shortage. Order or operation splitting is dividing a production lot into two or more parts to get the required number through more quickly to resolve a shortage. In all of these cases, the master scheduler must verify that there is still a feasible schedule for manufacturing with the changes implemented.

Customer orders

Customer orders are the backbone and foundation of manufacturing. All plans are developed and executed with the expectation of receiving and filling customer orders. Customer orders are entered through the customer order entry module, which is connected to the master scheduling process and thus manufacturing planning and control. Customer orders are one of the many inputs to the ongoing master scheduling process. The customer order entry module must be capable of receiving and holding more than simple one-time orders, but also the newer ordering methods like annual contracts and release systems associated with supplier partnerships. The available-to-promise (ATP) facility of master scheduling software tracks the products available per time period by comparing current inventory, planned production, and customer orders. This information allows sales representatives to make knowledgeable commitments to customers and stops them from committing to orders that cannot be filled.

Master Schedule Chart

A typical master schedule shows fields of information in chart form, in addition to individual pieces of information included in addition to the chart. The standard fields of data shown in the chart are the time periods projected, which is the top row identifying the time periods for which the other fields of data are shown; the demand forecast per product per time period; the number of customer orders already received per time period; the projected available balance at the end of each time period, including an insertion of the number available or balance on hand prior to the first time period shown; the quantity of items available to be promised to customers for that time period; and the master production schedule (MPS) quantity of items to be produced per time period.

Projected Available Balance

During the segment of the master schedule prior to the demand time fence, the projected available balance at the end of a given time period is calculated simply as the difference between the balance on hand, or projected available balance at the end of the previous time period, and the customer orders received for the time period in question. The formula reads as follows: projected available balance = balance on hand – customer orders received. Beyond the demand time fence in the planning time fence, the calculation is slightly more complex. The projected available balance at the end of a given time period is the difference between the balance on hand, or the projected available balance from the previous time period, and either the forecast demand or the customer orders received for that time period, whichever is higher. The formula reads as follows: projected available balance = balance on hand – (the higher of forecast demand or customer orders received).

Forecast Consumption

A product forecast is made as an estimate of the projected sales for a given time period. The production plan, master schedule, and master production schedule (MPS) all work toward the goal of having a sufficient quantity of product to meet the forecast sales. As actual customer orders come in, it is said that the forecast is consumed. Initially, there is a demand forecast but there are no customer orders. As the time period in question approaches, customer orders come in. As the orders come in, it is said that the forecast is being consumed. The portion of the demand forecast quantity that corresponds to the quantity of customer orders received is thus "spoken for" or consumed. The forecast is completely consumed when the quantity of customer orders received reaches the demand forecast quantity. Forecast consumption is closely related to the available-to-promise quantity.

Time-Phased Order Records

Time-phased order records refers to the practice of master production scheduling which is not parallel to the actual customer orders or anticipated demand for the given time periods due to a company's practice of stockpiling goods for peak periods in a seasonal demand pattern. In time periods experiencing lesser demand, production exceeds the forecast demand and actual sales in order to store goods for the pending peak period(s). In time periods experiencing greater demand, forecast demand and actual sales exceed production and the inventory built in preparation is used up to fill the remaining customer orders. This is similar the practice of level scheduling.

Frozen Period

In the frozen period, which extends from the beginning of the master production schedule to the demand time fence, final assembly occurs and manufacturing changes are costly and difficult to make. Materials and capacity are already committed, even partially spent. The manufacturing that occurs at this time is to meet customer demand, and changes will interfere with that objective. Customer orders requiring delivery within this period can be taken if there is a sufficient available-to-promise quantity in that period to fill the order, but usually changes made at this point require replacing one production order with another, resulting in lost output and unplanned costs. To actually change the scheduled production within this window requires approval from personnel at a higher level than the master scheduler; usually the company's chief executive officer (CEO), since changes will likely interfere with filling already promised customer orders and can cost the company money and good will.

Flexible Period

In the flexible period, which extends from the demand time fence to the planning time fence of the master production schedule (MPS), lower level manufacturing and purchasing occur. During this window, changes to the manufacturing schedule can occur with the approval of the master scheduler as long as there are sufficient materials and capacity available or sufficient materials and capacity can be made available. The changes must be made manually by the master scheduler, rather than routinely through the control system. Changes are often made possible by substituting one production order for another, which can be possible since the commitment is not as strong as it is in the frozen period. Changes are not always possible, though, since they may negatively affect material supply, capacity availability, customer deliveries, and cost. From the beginning of the master schedule until the planning time fence (the end of the flexible period) is the cumulative lead time for production.

Look-Ahead Period

The look-ahead period, which is also known as the batching period or free period, extends from the planning time fence to the planning horizon of the master production schedule (MPS). In the look-ahead period, low-level manufacturing components are obtained for future manufacturing according to the company's batching rules and both short-term and long-term capacity changes are planned. It is within this window that future plans are made and changed. Changes in manufacturing planning are made through routine entries into the manufacturing planning and control system. Material availability is not a problem, since there is time for purchasing. Capacity availability can be more problematic as planning occurs and the schedule fills up.

Product Structure Sample

```
   A
 __|__
 |   |
 1   B
   __|__
   |   |
   2   3
```

The product structure is simply the relationship that exists between a manufactured item and the raw materials and constituent parts used to manufacture it. The sample product structure describes the make-up of end item A. End item A is manufactured from raw materials numbers one, two, and three. In the lower level of manufacturing, constituent part B is processed from raw materials numbers two and three. In the higher level of manufacturing, constituent part B from the lower level of manufacturing is processed along with raw material number one to form the end item A. Raw materials numbers two and three are component parts of their parent part B. Similarly, raw material number one and constituent part B are component parts of their parent part end product A. (Constituent parts are also referred to as components, but that terminology has been avoided in this example to avoid confusion with the similar but different term component part; letters indicate fabricated parts and numbers indicate raw materials.)

PRODUCT STRUCTURE RECORD SAMPLE

Parent| Component| Quantity| On| Off| Phantom

Code| Code| Per| Date| Date| Indicator

A1| B2| 3| M/D/Y | M/D/Y| N

This product structure record exists for item B2. The record details the relationship of component part B2 to its parent part A1. Multiple product structure records can exist referencing parent part A1, each detailing the relationship of an individual component part, of which there is usually more than one, to the single parent part. From the sample product structure record, it is apparent that three component parts B2 are used in the fabrication of parent part A1. The product structure record also indicates the start and stop dates the product is used and whether the part is real or a phantom used for planning.

EXPLOSION AND IMPLOSION

An explosion of a bill of material (BOM) focuses on the production of the part referenced. The BOM information is displayed in a format that shows the lower level parts used to manufacture the referenced part. A BOM implosion focuses on the part itself and the parent parts it is used to build, rather than the parts of which it is made. Information is displayed for all production uses of the part, showing all the different parent parts the item is used in. In short, a BOM explosion shows how a particular part is built from other parts, and a BOM implosion shows all the ways a particular part is used to make other parts.

SINGLE-LEVEL BILL OF MATERIAL SAMPLE

```
          A
   _______|_______
   |    |    |    |
   1    2    B   C (3)
```

A bill of material (BOM) is a record that defines the make-up of the parent part referenced. Single-level BOM's provide only the immediately preceding level of construction. This sample BOM indicates that parent item A is constructed from raw materials one and two and constituent parts B and C. Numbers in parenthesis indicate the quantity of that raw material or parent part used, with no number in parentheses indicating the quantity of one. So, more specifically, parent part A is constructed from one each of raw materials one and two and constituent part B and three of constituent part C. Since this is a single-level BOM, additional BOM's for B and C must be consulted to determine the entire breakdown of the make-up of item A. Furthermore, item A itself may not be the end item, but a constituent part referenced in other single-level BOM's. (Letters indicate fabricated parts and numbers indicate raw materials.)

Multi-level Bill of Material Sample

```
      A
     _|_
    |   |
    1   B (2)
       _|_
      |   |
      2   3 (3)
```

A multi-level bill of material (BOM) indicates the entire make-up of an end item, all the way down to the lowest level of manufacturing. In this sample, end item A is made up of raw materials one, two, and three and constituent part B. The specific relationship between the parts is that constituent part B is manufactured from raw materials two and three, and then is processed along with raw material one to form end item A. The numbers in parentheses beside the components of item A indicate the quantity used in processing, with no number indicating a quantity of one. So, more specifically, three of raw material three and one of raw material two make up constituent part B; two of constituent part B and one of raw material one make up end item A. (Letters indicate fabricated parts and numbers indicate raw materials.)

Bill of Resources Sample

Product A Bill of Resources

Critical Resource| Time per unit in hours

10 Milling | 15.0

20 Drilling | 5.0

30 Packaging | 0.5

A bill of resources details the critical resources utilized in the production of an end item. This sample bill of resources indicates the processing necessary for the manufacture of product A. For each item A produced, fifteen hours of milling at work center ten, five hours of drilling at work center twenty, and a half hour of packaging at work center thirty are required. The bill does not include all of the processing necessary for item A, but only the portion of processing occurring at critical work centers requiring careful planning for a smooth flow through operations. A bill of labor is almost identical, except labor requirements by skill rather than critical resources would be listed.

Specialized Bills of Material

Bills of material (BOM's) can be formatted for particular applications. The overall file contains all of the related information, but specialized versions can be generated as desired. Two specific specializations commonly used are time and finance. For various reasons, the manufacturing and engineering functions may want BOM's for past, current, or future versions of the product. All of this information is retained in the system, and can be accessed and generated into a specialized BOM. Similarly, the finance function may want a BOM with standard costs or other financial information included. This information is also included in the system, and can be accessed and generated into a specialized BOM.

Bill of Labor

A bill of labor is a manufacturing record that depicts a structured table of the different types and amounts of labor necessary for the manufacture of one production unit of the product to which the bill applies. Bills of labor are used for planning purposes, primarily the determination of labor requirements for planned production per time period, but also resource and manufacturing family planning. A bill of labor is similar to a bill of resource, except that it details the required labor by skill rather than the resources necessary for production of the product referenced. Although resources utilized and labor required may seem overlapping, they are not necessarily identical.

RCCP

Rough-cut capacity planning (RCCP) is a tool used by the master scheduler to verify the feasibility of the master production schedule (MPS). Once a tentative MPS is generated, the production quantities and timing specified are compared to the applicable bills of resources and work center availability per time period. A load comparison is generated, from which the master scheduler can determine if the proposed loading is reasonable. This process is especially critical for the bottleneck work centers that cause manufacturing problems. RCCP is an iterative process, since the MPS loading is not generally feasible on the first version. The master scheduler considers the load comparison generated through RCCP, and makes appropriate changes to the MPS. This process is repeated until the load comparison indicates that the loading and thus the MPS are realistic. This overall process is obviously simpler in production environments with excess capacity.

The objectives of rough-cut capacity planning (RCCP) include checking the feasibility of the proposed master production schedule (MPS), avoiding work-in-process build-up through effective manufacturing management, predicting future utilization of critical work centers for planning purposes, and indicating possible manufacturing bottlenecks and the severity of these bottlenecks early on so they can be prevented. Additionally, RCCP can indicate future tooling requirements for manufacturing if the bills of resources include the necessary tools as well as planning capacity requirements for suppliers if they are included in the system as critical work centers.

The outputs of rough-cut capacity planning (RCCP) are typically capacity charts and load profiles. The capacity charts can be formulated to display the individual resource requirements per product, the total individual resources requirements, and the availability of individual resources. These charts are generated per time period, and overloading is easily spotted through discrepancies between the totals required and the availability. Alternatively, capacity charts can be formulated to display the total required individual resources per time period over a range of time periods and the corresponding resource availability. In this format, requirement and availability discrepancies are also easily detected. Load profiles are graphs of the number of standard hours required per time period. These graphs apply to one resource or work center. Requirements entered on the graph that exceed the availability are quickly detected visually.

Capacity planning using overall factors (CPOF) is a rough-cut capacity planning technique (RCCP) in which engineered time standards are not employed, but rather the actual build time required for the MPS schedule is calculated and broken down among the required work centers. The items and quantities included on the master schedule are multiplied by the total build time for each item, resulting in the number of hours necessary to produce the schedule. These required production hours are then broken down among the work centers based on historical percentages, indicating the total number of hours per work center necessary to complete the master schedule. This schedule of hours per work center required by time period is evaluated through trial runs. The CPOF process must be repeated whenever a new time period is added to the master schedule or when the master schedule or MPS is changed.

FAS

The sequential steps involved in developing a final assembly schedule (FAS) are as follows: determination of the FAS horizon, or the extent into the future for which final assembly planning occurs, which should be short enough to provide customer responsiveness but long enough to complete the final build in response to customer orders; selection of the unit of measure (UOM) by which the product is defined, which is dependent on the production environment, often modules for discrete items and volumes for process manufacturing; and finally, determination of the priority sequencing rules, or the order in which final assembly of products is accomplished.

Since final assembly schedules (FAS's) are used to customize goods according to customer specifications in make-to-order and assemble-to-order production environments, the items being assembled are not identical but rather variable. The ordered flow of material into and along the assembly line is crucial. Both internal and external suppliers are notified along with manufacturing of the fixed sequence of units, and supplied materials must be in the specified sequence. The order of manufacturing as well as the order of products manufactured are set and must be adhered to by all parties concerned for a successful outcome.

The final assembly schedule (FAS) and the master schedule for a given manufacturing operation are in constant contact. There is an ongoing flow of information both ways between the two schedules. The forecast demand data, both quantities and options, is maintained in the master schedule. Customer orders are entered through the order entry module into the FAS, which then flow back to the master schedule. The current available-to-promise data is held on the master schedule, but is partially determined by the current customer order information passed from the FAS. The two schedules are so closely connected that it is not uncommon for the master scheduler to also control the order entry into the FAS.

The key to making delivery promises is the availability of the necessary capacity and materials. The steps involved in delivery promising logic are as follows: identification of customer requirements, which occurs at the time of order entry and is entered into the system as actual demand replacing or consuming available, "un-slotted" forecast demand; determination of the available capacity, since the actual demand and the forecast demand which has been planned do not necessarily line up; determination of the available components, since the actual demand and the forecast demand which has been planned do not necessarily line up; and the determination of the quantity available to promise, which is not necessarily straightforward when it comes to customizations.

The final assembly capacity is a limiting factor on production output. The forecast of final assembly schedule (FAS) options is translated into standard hours of resources required for their manufacture, which establishes the normal load for final assembly per time period. Unfortunately, the actual loading does not necessarily correspond to the normal forecast loading due to fluctuations and seasonality. Load leveling is not a good solution in this situation since the point of the FAS is to assemble goods quickly in response to customer orders. It is better to design the final assembly process to handle peak periods, providing extra capacity beyond the normal forecast load to meet peak demand. Minimizing FAS lead times is also helpful.

The final assembly material supply is a limiting factor on production output. Manufacturing components, including raw materials and purchased and internally manufactured parts, are supplied for the final assembly schedule (FAS) according to master scheduled quantities and options forecasting with planning bill breakdowns. As customer orders are received, the available-to-promise (ATP) facility of the master scheduling system is accessed and utilized to determine availability of components to meet the actual demand. The success of the ATP facility is dependent on the accuracy and completeness of the bills of material referenced in the master schedule, since these are the basis for ordering production supplies.

The standard available-to-promise quantity is calculated as the quantity on hand at the beginning of the time period minus the demand until the next MPS output. When options and customizations are available, the ATP calculation becomes more complex. The overall ATP quantity for the unit remains the same. The ATP quantity for the specific options and customizations is calculated as the percentage of the overall ATP quantity specified for the option in the planning bills. As the overall and options ATP quantities are consumed by actual customer orders, the two must be reconciled. The individual options ATP quantities cannot exceed the overall unit ATP quantity. Even though supplies for a particular option may exceed the units available, that option cannot be supplied on more units than are available.

PRIORITY SYSTEMS

When a company has planned more manufacturing than can be completed by the given deadlines and the deadlines are found to be non-negotiable, priority systems are used to determine the re-planning process. If not all customer needs can be met, than it must be determined which customer needs will be met. One priority system is an ABC customer rating system. Customers are rated according to the volume and frequency of their orders, or the level of commitment between the customer and supplier. The A-rated customers are given first priority in rescheduling, followed by B-rated customers and then C-rated customers. Alternatively, companies may prioritize profit. The products that generate the most profit for the company are given priority in rescheduling. The actual priority system used varies from company to company and must be determined in the sales and operations planning meeting so that the master scheduler and planners know how to proceed.

SCHEDULE VALIDITY

SCHEDULE REVIEW

Maintaining a realistic, effective master schedule is the key to improving master schedule validity. Once the schedule becomes unrealistic or ineffective, it is invalid. One tool to maintain the master schedule is master schedule review. The master schedule should be reviewed on a regular basis, usually weekly, in a meeting including the master scheduler and manufacturing, sales, planning, and materials personnel. The purpose of the meeting is to review the master schedule and identify and resolve any problems as they develop. The problems must be addressed immediately in order to minimize their impact on the master schedule, production, and customer service. If the master schedule is not reviewed for problems and the problems resolved, then the problems get worse as time passes and they affect other levels of production and ultimately customer service.

LEAD TIME REDUCTION

Shorter lead times provide greater flexibility, lower work in process, and shorter forecasting horizons. Lead times can be reduced through eliminating waste, in particular time-consuming but unnecessary and non-value adding activities. Setup reduction, batch size reduction, work cell-based production, and just-in-time manufacturing are all good ways to reduce lead time. In addition to lead time reduction, lead time accuracy is an important consideration. The standard lead times used in calculations must reflect the actual lead times experienced, or the master schedule can break down. Both the lead time itself and the accuracy of the standard lead times must be monitored and improved.

FLATTENING

Flattening bills of material (BOM's) involves the minimization of manufacturing stopping points. With the exception of raw materials and purchased parts, each BOM component part is a manufacturing stopping point involving parts that are fabricated, stored, and then used later in production. Phantom bills and work cells are two ways to flatten BOM's, or minimize the stopping points. Phantom bills define items that are constructed but not stored and flow directly into the next operation or work cell. Work cells involve continuous flow through manufacturing. The work cell flow can be marked by pay points or counting points, at which components are considered complete, but continue in the manufacturing flow rather than being inventoried. Flattening BOM's decreases processing steps and inventory time, thus reducing lead time and cost.

Performance Measurements

Performance measurements relevant to the master schedule include the percentage of master production schedule (MPS) orders completed on time, the percentage of customer orders that are later changed by the customer, the percentage of MPS orders changed due to material shortages, and the percentage of MPS orders changed due to insufficient capacity. On-time completion is a measurement of the overall effectiveness of the MPS, while the others help pinpoint problem areas that may need to be addressed. High percentages of customer changes may prompt the development of a flexible manufacturing system to accommodate the customers, while high percentages of incomplete orders due to material shortages or capacity insufficiencies pinpoint internal and/or supplier problems that need to be resolved. When applied and executed appropriately, these performance measurements aid in the process of maintaining a valid master schedule.

Sales and Productions Plans

The outputs of the sales and operations planning process are the sales and production plans. As in all aspects of manufacturing, the effectiveness of these plans must be monitored so improvements can be made and the company can remain competitive. The sales plan is judged by how accurately actual sales are predicted, so actual sales are compared to forecast sales. The production plan is judged by the manufacturing output, so the actual quantities produced are compared to the production plan, via the master production schedule (MPS) and the master schedule. Adjustments can then be made as necessary. Some specific performance measures relevant to sales and operations planning performance are the percentage of the master production schedule (MPS) by number of manufacturing orders completed on time, the percentage of final assembly schedule (FAS) units completed on time, the percentages of MPS items changed inside the demand and planning time fences, the fulfillment rate of customer promises based on the available-to-promise (ATP) facility, and the overall fulfillment rate of customer promises.

Customer Service Department

The customer service department serves as a liaison between a company's manufacturing operations and their external customers. Both customers and manufacturing personnel communicate with, gain information from, and make decisions through customer service. When production problems arise, manufacturing approaches customer service to resolve the problem in accordance with customer needs. When customers require delivery promises, confirmation, or changes to an existing order, they approach the customer service department who agrees or negotiates based on manufacturing feasibility. The customer service department is in communication with both manufacturing personnel and the external customers, so that problems on either side can be resolved with due consideration to the other side.

Stock Out Percentage

The stock out percentage is a measurement of a company's effectiveness in meeting customer orders. The stock out percentage is the percentage of total orders or order line items that result in a stock out when filled, during a given time period. In relationship to the customer service ratio, the formula for calculating the stock out percentage is as follows: stock out percentage = (1 – customer service ratio) * 100, where the customer service ratio is defined as the percentage of orders, order line items, or order dollar amounts filled on schedule for a given time period.

IMPORTANT TERMS

Master schedule – A time-phased production planning chart including supply, demand, and available inventory master production schedule (MPS) – The specific, detailed production schedule derived from the master schedule.

Master scheduler – The staff person responsible for developing, reviewing, revising, managing, and maintaining a company's master schedule or the master schedule for particular items; the master scheduler should have significant experience in products, production, processing, and marketing because of the impact on customer service and material and capacity planning.

Master scheduling – The ongoing process whereby the master schedule is developed, reviewed, and adjusted to verify that inventory levels, customer service goals, and proper material and capacity planning are maintained; adjustments made to the master schedule must flow downstream to the master production schedule (MPS), as well.

Standard bill of material – A record of the make-up of a manufactured item or subassembly specifying the component parts (raw materials, piece parts, and/or subassemblies) of the parent (the part for which the record exists).

Planning bill – A record in the format of a bill of material that contains information used in planning material supply and manufacturing.

Super bill – A type of planning bill specifying the mix or spread of annual sales of a product family over the individual items within that family or customization options within a single item; super bills are used in combination with forecast data for the product family or customizable item to forecast and master schedule production of the individual items in the product family or the customization options within the individual product; super bills are also called percentage bills or family bills.

Product structure – A record detailing the total combined make-up of a manufactured item by combining the applicable bills of material (the bills of material themselves are only one level); a multi-level bill of material.

Common parts bill – A planning bill used to simplify planning and scheduling when many similar end items are produced; a common parts bill specifies the portion of the similar products that is identical, in order to plan and schedule that portion together and simplify master scheduling; the individual bills of material for the end items then refers to the common parts bill; common parts bills are also called phantom bills since they do not actually describe a product, but are an artificial construction to simplify planning.

Frozen period – The segment of future manufacturing planning from the current time until the demand time fence in which final manufacturing occurs ensuring the current period's promise dates; changes are not generally made in the frozen period; the frozen period can also be referred to as the final assembly period.

Flexible period – The segment of future manufacturing planning from the demand time fence until the planning time fence in which purchasing and lower level manufacturing will occur; changes can be made during the flexible period by the master scheduler as available material and capacity allow.

Free period – The segment of future manufacturing planning from the planning time fence until the planning horizon in which inventory is replenished for future production and long-term changes are planned.

Hedging – the practice of securing supplies in advance in order to avoid future fluctuations in price, quality, or availability; in the case of stabilizing master schedules, hedging usually involves the timing rather than the pricing of the supplies: supplies are secured earlier than necessary to avoid any anticipated problems and guarantee their availability on planned manufacturing start dates.

Options over-planning – the practice of purposefully exceeding the demand forecast by padding inventory of options with unpredictable demand patterns in order to protect against forecast inaccuracies and demand instabilities; options over-planning is specific and targeted, and thus differs from general overstocking.

Safety stock – a finished goods inventory buffer whose quantity is calculated using the statistical safety stock formulation with the customer service level agreed upon in the sales and operations planning meeting and utilized to protect against demand variation.

Safety capacity – the availability of more manufacturing capability than is necessary to fulfill the planned workload in order to handle unanticipated capacity demands due to work imbalances, rework, maintenance, equipment malfunctions, etc.; safety capacity decreases lead times and quantities of work in process, increases competitiveness, and allows target completion dates to be met even when problems occur.

Safety lead time – a time offset used in scheduling deliveries from consistently unreliable suppliers in order to receive materials when they are actually needed; the order delivery date is set at the usual late interval ahead of when the order is actually needed for manufacturing so that the necessary goods arrive on time or possibly early rather than late.

Linear programming – A mathematical technique used to determine the relationship between multiple variables, usually limited resources that will produce the desired result, usually maximum profit or minimum cost.

Advanced planning and scheduling (APS) system – A computerized system that receives input from the standard manufacturing control system and uses finite loading techniques to generate a revised and more detailed plan; APS systems replace infinite capacity requirements planning (CRP) and are utilized by many world-class production organizations.

Pegging – The availability within material requirements planning (MRP) and the master production schedule (MPS) of the parent-component relationship information of included materials; active, where-used information related to the specified parts.

Bottom-up re-planning – The process of revising the manufacturing plan in response to material shortages based on the actual material availability and what end items can be produced with those available materials; bottom-up re-planning relies heavily on pegging data.

Product code – The identification number(s) and/or letter(s) that indicate(s) the item to which the master schedule information applies; the product code is also called the item code.

Lead time – The time required for the level of manufacturing and/or assembly planned in the master schedule.

Lot size – The number of the items in question which are produced in one manufacturing batch; the lot size is also called the batch size.

Quantity on hand – The number of items in question available in stock prior to the commencement of the master schedule.

Demand time fence – The point in time before which manufacturing plans are frozen and cannot be changed lightly or easily so that the immediate demand for product can be met.

Planning time fence – The point in time beyond the demand time fence before which and after the demand time fence production planning occurs into the future.

Component part – A raw material, constituent part, or other manufacturing element that is used to fabricate or assemble another part (its parent part), either the end item or some intermediate.

Parent part – A component part, intermediate assembly, or final product made from raw materials, constituent parts, and/or other manufacturing elements (components); a part that is made from other parts is the parent part to those other parts.

Product structure – The process flow for a parent part, including constituent parts, their quantities, and how they are put together to form the parent.

Product structure record – A computerized record of the product structure detailing the relationship of a part to its parent; all parts used to produce a parent part have a product structure record detailing the relationship to the parent and other related information.

Final assembly schedule (FAS) – A manufacturing planning and control technique utilized in make-to-order and assemble-to-order production environments in order to increase manufacturing flexibility and meet customer specifications quickly; in final assembly scheduling, modules are master scheduled and stored and then customized end products are built according to the FAS from the modules after specific customer orders are received; demand is forecasted for the quantities of items to be built, and planning bills specifying option breakdowns are used for planning customizations.

Order slotting – The practice of planning a final assembly rate of production, supplied according to a planning bill, and then filling the planned production with the customer orders received; the FAS is limited by the planned production and option quantities; quantities and options ordered beyond the available slots can be deferred until a future time period with open slots.

CPIM Practice Test

Want to take this practice test in an online interactive format?
Check out the online resources page, which includes interactive practice questions and much more: **mometrix.com/resources719/cpimmpr**

1. The feasibility of a master planning schedule may be tested:

a. By calculating ATP
b. By the process of trial and error
c. By the process of RCCP
d. The cumulative with look-ahead method

2. The practice of comparing graphic or tabular representations of manufacturing capacity with available hours for manufacture is called:

a. ATP
b. MRP
c. RCCP
d. CRP

3. When a material planning supervisor speaks of maintaining the validity of the material plan, it means that:

a. The initial recommendations for scheduling production must be adhered to
b. Orders are replanned as necessary in response to external changes
c. Production schedules must be approved by shop floor persons
d. Only accurate materials planning schedules must be used

4. A measure of the available quantities of finished product that can be used to fill current customer orders is termed:

a. ATP
b. RCCP
c. MPS
d. MRP

5. In order to sustain an efficient system of MRP through IT software, it is recommended that data integrity be maintained at a %age-rate minimum of:

a. 99%
b. 89%
c. 79%
d. 100%

6. MRP II systems were developed because:

a. A corporation may store its inventory in more than one factory location
b. Electronic communications were not efficient in early MRP applications
c. In original MRP versions, MRP did not include capacity planning
d. Of all of the above

7. A manufacturing corporation relies on a PAC system in order to:

a. Release production orders to the manufacturing shop
b. Establish priorities and production sequences with the data from daily dispatch lists and work release orders
c. Monitor input/output and make corrections to the scheduling of material and work in the production sequences
d. All of the above

8. FAS may be functionally defined by which of the following?

a. Final assembly schedule
b. Full assembly status
c. A final assembly schedule that completes manufacture regardless of existing demand
d. A postponement of finished product until it can be matched with customer demand

9. Which of the following choices represents the best example of FAS in the auto industry?

a. The choice of engine size
b. The choice of model, color, and trim level
c. The choice of luxury sound systems
d. The choice of dashboard configuration

10. The MPS, or master production schedule, is based upon:

a. Demand forecast data, trends, and seasonality
b. Market research figures
c. Quantity, configuration, and completion dates
d. Flow line configuration, available personnel, and materials

11. Comparing the master schedule (MS) with the master production schedule (MPS), one might say that the:

a. MPS does not address quantities, product groups, or completed inventory, whereas the MS does
b. MS is broader and more general and includes many of the planning elements that are absent from the MPS
c. MPS includes demand forecasts and backlogged items for which customer orders have been received
d. MS is essentially the output from the MPS

12. The best argument for including a plan for supply chain postponement (FAS) in the master schedule is best demonstrated in which of the following examples?

a. The manufacture of replica sports team jackets and jerseys.
b. The manufacture of fluorescent lighting fixtures.
c. The manufacture of flooring materials.
d. The manufacture of beauty supplies.

13. Master scheduling includes demand forecasts, and in the case of athletic replica clothing, production would most likely be focused upon:

a. Capacity, material supply and commodity prices
b. Quantity, product groupings, and safety stock
c. Seasonality, player trades, and free agent signings
d. Make-to-order, make-to-stock, and buffer stock

14. The minimum time for the MS planning horizon should be as long as the:

a. Master production schedule
b. Engineering and procurement time
c. Lead time required to fabricate the items on the master schedule
d. Time required for production and delivery to the customer

15. The statement that best explains the difference between periodic and perpetual inventory accounting is:

a. Distributors of high-volume retail products must adhere to perpetual inventory accounting methods, while manufacturers must take advantage of the cost savings in period inventory accounting
b. Periodic inventory is better suited to MRP; perpetual inventory accounting methods are not
c. Periodic inventory accounting does not individually account for all purchases and releases but only occasionally counts inventory on hand; perpetual inventory accounting logs in every receipt and release of inventory stock
d. Perpetual inventory systems can be used only in manufacturing smaller lots of high-priced products; large economy-of-scale manufacture must rely on periodic inventory accounting

16. RRP, or resource requirements planning, is often said to be an integrated program involving:

a. Software that explores inventory reduction plans
b. Software that models production control plans
c. Software that supports and monitors the inventory reduction and production control plans
d. Software that controls materials routing

17. During the first MPS period of a product manufacture, the ATP quantity would be:

a. Zero
b. The beginning inventory
c. The sum of customer orders completed before the next MPS receipt
d. The projected available balance

18. In its beginning stage, a production plan is:

a. A list of required capacity and vital resources needed for manufacture
b. An authorization by operations-level management of a specific MPS
c. A combined sales and operations plan stated in terms of product or product groups
d. A projected level of customer demand

19. Why is the Japanese concept of kanban so important in lean manufacturing?

a. Because it reduces inventory costs
b. Because it is a "pull" system
c. Because it does not require computers
d. Because it exposes otherwise hidden problems

20. The part of the master schedule that designates the work centers that will be utilized for manufacture is:

a. The operations schedule
b. The job schedule
c. The master production schedule
d. The general plan

21. Operations scheduling is different from job scheduling in that:

a. Operations scheduling is a longer-term plan that assigns start and end dates to production orders
b. Operations scheduling breaks the job down into separate tasks and work stations
c. Operations scheduling determines the work centers to be used
d. Job scheduling is a longer-term plan for assigning start and end dates to production orders

22. Bottlenecks, excess inventory, and unresponsive manufacturing can be best addressed by:

a. Minimized material handling
b. Matching capacity to demand
c. More accurate production scheduling
d. Synchronization of the production process

23. In the master planning process, planners have plenty of room to improve on the estimated 10% of throughput efficiency. How can throughput efficiency be calculated?

a. Value Added Time ÷ End to End Pipeline Time × 100
b. Value Added Time × End to End Pipeline Time ÷ 100
c. End to End Pipeline Time ÷ 100 × Value Added Time
d. End to End Pipeline Time × 100 ÷ Value Added Time

24. How are subassemblies handled on a computerized BOM?

a. Subassemblies are broken down into separate entry items
b. Subassemblies are attached in separate BOMs
c. Subassemblies are entered as single items on the BOM
d. Subassemblies are not entered on the BOM

25. What are the two levels of MRP output?

a. Purchase orders and reschedule notices
b. Data integration and FAS
c. Recommended production schedule and recommended purchasing schedule
d. Single layer and parent level output

26. Arrange the following manufacturing steps in the proper sequential order: production control; master production schedule; capacity requirements planning; and materials requirements planning using their appropriate abbreviations:

a. CRP, MPS, PC, and MRP
b. MPS, MRP, CRP, and PC
c. MRP, MPS, CRP, and PC
d. PC, MPS, CRP, and MRP

27. ERP, or enterprise resource planning, is best described as:

a. A process developed in the 1970s that transformed manufacturing into a streamlined process
b. A process developed in the 1960s that used a production planning and inventory management process to manage manufacturing
c. The latest in a series of manufacturing innovations that integrates an entire company organization into a single central operations information module
d. All of the above

28. Cost management in planning applies to which of the following areas?

a. Auditing of the company balance sheet
b. Assessing speculative changes in labor, material, and overhead
c. Accounting for specific material costs of supplied materials
d. Computing net asset value of the corporation

29. The planning process for manufacturing should include an FMEA analysis. FMEA is best described as:

a. A method of analyzing the planned manufacturing schedule to determine where failures are likely to occur.
b. An analysis of the efficiency of inventory location in the supply chain.
c. A method of scoring failure risk in the supply chain.
d. A Frequency of Materials Emergency Analysis

30. Among the things that most impact planning in the global supply chain is:

a. Competition for commodities
b. Political instability in supplier countries
c. Economic instability and currency fluctuations in supplier countries
d. All of the above

31. In the materials planning stage of a global corporation, political and economic instability in the global supply chain can be best addressed by:

a. Concentrating all materials and component purchasing into a single supplier
b. Diversifying supply sources among several suppliers and even different supplier countries
c. Having the financial department involved in buying commodity options
d. All of the above

32. The best example of a case in which commodity fluctuation risk caused by economic instability can impact supply chain planning is:

a. An aluminum door and window frame manufacturer has not integrated financial planning into master planning
b. An auto manufacturer has a five-year contract with the world's most successful supplier of aluminum alloy wheels
c. An aluminum foil manufacturer hedges its raw materials position
d. An aluminum cooking utensil manufacturer has an oversupply of inventory on the shop floor

33. The best example of material commodities price risk to the supply chain can be found in which of the following?

a. Hex bolts
b. Auto transmissions
c. Window glass
d. Aluminum

34. In master planning of resources, demand management is the process of:

a. Forecasting demand and distributing resources
b. Ensuring that there is enough supply to meet demand
c. Establishing the master production schedule in accordance with demand
d. Forecasting, order entry and promising, and prioritizing customer orders when products are in short supply

35. A WMS, or warehouse management system, employs AIDC technology. The AIDC process utilizes:

a. Hand trolleys, tow motors, bins, and floor jacks
b. Shipping, receiving, stacking, and picking
c. Barcode scanners and RFID
d. All of the above

36. At what stage of the MPC process would sales and operations planning occur?

a. Sales and operations planning would occur at the operations management planning level
b. Sales and operations planning would occur at the top management planning stage
c. Sales and operations planning would occur simultaneously with that of the operations management execution plan
d. Sales and operations planning would occur at the level of the operations management execution plan

37. At what stage of the MPC process would schedule and capacity requirements planning occur?

a. Scheduling and capacity requirements planning would occur at the OMP, or operations management planning, level
b. Scheduling and capacity requirements planning would occur at the top management planning level
c. Scheduling and capacity requirements planning would occur at the level of the operations management execution plan
d. Scheduling and capacity requirement planning would occur at all levels of management operational levels

38. Materials planners may establish a fixed safety stock in manufacturing planning situations where:

a. Supplier dependability is in question
b. A still popular product has a well-known demand curve
c. Holiday demand requires higher-volume manufacturing of the product
d. Products are either completely new or being phased out

39. Time period safety stock __________.

a. Is used when a product is being phased out
b. Is equal to the forecast usage of inventory multiplied by the length of the time period for which the safety stock is valid
c. Stays the same even when demand changes
d. Is used when supply reliability is stable and uniform

40. Among the ways in which productive capacity can be adjusted to meet different conditions and demand is by:

a. Adding more workers or decreasing the workforce
b. Adding or removing of work centers
c. Rescheduling of manufacturing orders
d. All of the above

41. In CRP applied to workers, currently available employee hours can be computed by:

a. Adding employee hours for released manufacturing orders to the total of all available employee hours
b. Adding all available employee hours to the %age of employee capacity used for released manufacturing orders
c. Subtracting employee hours used for released manufacturing orders from all available employee hours
d. Subtracting employee hours used for released manufacturing orders from all available machine hours

42. In planning production schedules, post-operation production time must be factored into planning. The best definition of post-operation time is:

a. The time required to set up a new manufacturing process
b. The time required to move finished products to ATP inventory
c. A required waiting time before unfinished products can move to the next stage of manufacturing
d. A required waiting time before finished products can be logged into finished inventory

43. Define the term manufacturing instruction.

a. A manufacturing instruction contains the same information as a routing sheet.
b. A manufacturing instruction is a planning diagram.
c. A manufacturing instruction determines the direction of work flow.
d. A manufacturing instruction contains more detailed information than can be found on the routing sheet.

44. Define work center data and tell why these data are important in MP.

a. Work center data consist of information collected at specific work centers; they can be used to set man-hours required at the station
b. Work center data are an inventory monitoring system that measures MTBFs (mean-time-between failures)
c. Work center data are a compilation of employee hours and machine hours; they can be used to measure the efficiency of a manufacturing system
d. Work center data are the computer output of capacity and control information at work centers; they are important in materials planning because they offer critical intelligence to the planning and design of future manufacturing

45. A consumer-driven product with a short life cycle and an unpredictable and volatile demand would most likely be manufactured:

a. By the automotive industry
b. By the fashion industry
c. By the commodity industry
d. By a maker of large mainframe computers

46. Basic layout formations in manufacturing can be process layout, cell layout, product layout, and a hybrid mix of the preceding types. In terms of planning, the best characterization of the cellular or cell layout is:

a. Cellular layouts are often a preferred layout for producing a specific part or parts that have the same resource requirements; cell layouts are treated as a single unit with regard to work center files and routing sheets
b. Cellular layouts are traditional lean-style modified assembly line processes
c. Cellular layouts are suitable for producing small batches of product families in a variety of complex configurations
d. Cellular layouts are the best planning choice for building large products like boats, airplanes, and commercial earthmoving or excavation equipment; cell layouts must be accompanied by detailed and separate routing sheets and work center files

47. Process engineering planning for a cellular layout would likely include:

a. Flow charts showing external handling of materials
b. Product selection, tool numbers, and flow charts
c. Demand forecasting, materials purchasing, and MRO
d. Equipment selection, setup times, assembly times, and labor

48. Operations management planning is the next step after top-level management has created a general plan for sales, operations, business, and resource requirements planning. Operations management planning consists of:

a. Capacity planning, material requirements planning, and production scheduling, but not distribution planning
b. Capacity planning, materials requirements planning, production scheduling, and distribution planning
c. Materials requirements planning, production scheduling, and distribution planning, but not capacity planning
d. Production scheduling, capacity planning, and distribution planning, but not materials requirements planning

49. The master schedule horizon is divided by time fences. This means that:

a. The master schedule horizon is divided into separate time periods consisting of the final assembly stage, the manufacturing and purchasing stage, and the look-ahead period
b. Time fences are used to prove the feasibility of the master production schedule
c. The master schedule horizon is divided into separate time periods consisting of rough-cut capacity planning, distribution planning, and materials resource planning
d. The master schedule horizon is separated into two time fences—a manufacturing and purchasing stage and a look-ahead period

Answer Key and Explanations

1. C: Answer option "c" is the correct answer. The means for testing the feasibility of a master planning schedule is found in RCCP, or rough-cut capacity planning. RCCP operates much like an early warning system and is helpful in preventing bottlenecks from developing. The RCCP method is useful in quantifying and gauging the size of problems likely to arise from customer demand, productive capacity, and inventory planning. The data obtained from RCCP can flow to all work centers, including those involved in supply and production, and make it easier to match productive capacity to the master planning schedule.

2. D: The correct answer is "d," capacity requirements planning. CRP retrieves the order data from MRP. Using graphic or table representations of capacity and comparing those with hours available for manufacture gives a more precise account of material and capacity requirements needed to meet customer orders to the required specifications. In the CRP process, each manufacturing step is isolated, with the total number of operations at each work station multiplied by average run times.

3. B: The best answer is "b" (although it would be nice if "only accurate materials planning schedules" could be used... The demand and production environment is always changing, and a good materials planning operation should permit of the flexibility necessary to accommodate change. A properly detailed materials planning process also includes replanning alternatives and alternate scheduling. Maintaining the validity of a material plan involves setting priorities, the use of modeling and what-if scenarios, and replanning to fit the changing environment.

4. A: ATP means available-to-promise, and is a measure of the amount of finished product that can be used to meet existing customer demand. In order to be counted as ATP, finished products must be available for delivery within the customer's specified delivery date. ATP is usually incorporated into information technology software and is usually based upon push or pull production models. MPS refers to the master production schedule; MRP means materials requirements planning; RCCP refers to rough-cut capacity planning.

5. A: The correct answer is "a." The entire purpose of materials requirements planning is to maintain lean manufacturing through lean inventories and delivery of materials to the right place at the right time. Most MRP software aims for 99% accuracy in the bill of materials, inventory data, and the master production scheduling. Common errors in inputting data to MRP software systems is inaccuracy in calculating lead times, particularly in failing to recognize outside factors that can skew results—such as other products being made within the same factory.

6. C: All of the above have a degree of validity, but the best answer is "c." It is true that inefficient communications from factory to factory and from factory to supplier are essential to a good MRP system. However, the key factor missing from early MRP operations was that it did not take manufacturing capacity (and its variations) into consideration. MRP II is more inclusive of such things as finance and human relations factors.

7. D: The correct answer is "d." PAC, or production activity control, does all of these things and more. Since PAC provides electronic information collection of input and output data, it is the ideal mechanism for making corrections to the production system. A PAC system monitors work in progress and completed orders and reports production that is delayed or bottlenecked. A properly calibrated PAC applies the right measures of resources, equipment, and material to the manufacturing process.

8. D: The correct answer is "d." The idea behind FAS, or the final assembly schedule, is to keep the inventory of finished supply lean until it can be matched with customer demand. FAS are typically implemented in the manufacture of products that have different variations or are produced in "sets." The manufacture of toy teddy bears may be finished in different textures, fabrics, or colors, for example. Another example would be in a set of cosmetics or other beauty supplies.

9. B: The best answer among the choices provided is "b," the choice of model, color, and trim level. Although market research data will tell such information as what colors are most popular, it is best to postpone final assembly until there are customer orders that can be matched to factory production final assembly, in order to prevent excess inventory and carry charges. The use of trim levels and "models" can be deferred until orders come in, with the basic auto having already been built complete with frames, suspensions, engines, drive chains, and other vital components. Such things as color and trim level are selective and can be matched to customer order preference.

10. C: The best answer is "c." The master production schedule is a set of figures and projections that are specific with regard to the configuration of product groups to be manufactured, the quantities to be built, and the target dates for beginning and completion of manufacture. While MPS does take into account the more subjective areas of demand forecast figures, availability of material, and management policies, the MPS is anchored in the specifics of manufacture. Also figuring prominently in the MPS will be pipeline and standard inventory.

11. B: Answer "b" is correct. The master schedule is broader and more general than the master production schedule, and includes many of the planning elements that are absent from the MPS. The MS incorporates forecast demand, customer backlogs, and the plan for supplying the manufacture, on-hand demand, and ATP. The MPS is often termed the "nuts and bolts" of the manufacturing process and delivers specifics with regard to start and stop dates, quantities to be manufactured, and the composition of manufacturing sets or product groupings.

12. A: The best answer is "a." None of the alternatives argues better for including a supply chain postponement into manufacturing plans and schedules. The manufacture of replica sports team jackets and jerseys is a volatile business, greatly influenced by the movement of star athletes between teams, popularity of teams vis à vis win-loss records, and a variety of other popularity factors. New York Yankee "Jeter" jerseys would lose value in inventory if the celebrity player moved to another team. The other choices have little or no variety, excepting beauty supplies, where the challenge is more one of "kitting" than postponement.

13. C: The best answer is "c." The highly profitable business of manufacturing celebrity athletic and team clothing also has a volatility that can eat into profits. While marketing research tools can provide baseline data for consumption, this kind of data collection cannot determine which teams or players are going to sell the most replica sports apparel, nor which players are drafted or traded. Seasonality is a big factor in replica sports apparel, since a large portion of it is sold during the Christmas season. In creating a master schedule, and deriving from it the master production schedule for NFL material, it would be well to consider the lull typically occurring between February and April.

14. C: The correct answer is "c," and it must be noted that the MS planning horizon lead time includes product design and materials procurement time. The master production schedule is chiefly concerned with the stages of actual production—the "nuts and bolts" of the manufacturing process. The master schedule, in most cases, sets the rate of manufacture in a more general way, either by hour or by length of shift, and so it must encompass more than the sum total of all production phases.

15. C: The correct choice is "c." There are good reasons why one business might choose periodic inventory accounting and why another might prefer perpetual inventory accounting, but all of them have to do with costs and efficiencies. Traditionally, perpetual accounting was the province of small-lot high priced product manufacture but scanning and computer equipment have extended this option to all producers. But the differences between the two methods are clearly explained in answer choice "c."

16. C: The best answer is "c." The "integrated" part of the question provides a clue, referring to the fact that RPP software supports and monitors the plans for lean manufacturing through inventory reduction and by information technology, which supports efficient production. Properly implemented, the RPP software will integrate workloads, production scheduling, and materials routing and will set reliable lead times. Resource requirements planning modules are customized to fit circumstances in the particular manufacturing environment.

17. B: The correct answer is "b." ATP refers to the quantity of finished product available for delivery to the customer within a specified period of time. During the first MPS period of manufacture, the only "available to promise" quantity would be the beginning inventory or on-hand balance. With production under way, the available-to-promise inventory is subject to change. However, it must be noted that ATP, compiled in lots or batches, can be reduced only by customer orders received prior to receipt of the next master production schedule.

18. C: In its initial stage, the production plan combines sales forecasts and operations planning into a single action plan that describes product output at a monthly rate. The production plan precedes management authorization of the final master production schedule, which is subject to additional steps. Required capacity and key resources that are needed are part of the production plan, but that answer does not mention sales forecasting, a key component of the production plan. Production planning supports profitability objectives and the sales plan.

19. D: Answer choice "d" points to the single most important reason for keeping the supply chain lean using kanban techniques. Excess inventory disguises the real problems, particularly in assembly style manufacturing. The other answer choices are true but only tell part of the picture. Insofar as computerization goes, most modern lean manufacturing is controlled by a form of computerized kanban, though the traditional basic systems of "pulling" supply from upstream still works in many situations. Of course, inventory cost control is always a concern, but large savings can result from getting to the route of the problem. Removing excess inventory and bottlenecks can reveal hidden problems with capacity, equipment, and human resources.

20. B: The correct choice is answer "b." The job schedule is the part of the master schedule that designates the work centers used for the manufacture of a product or family of products. The master production schedule is a general plan that materials, material process, and labor estimates to materials issue transactions. At this stage, scheduling is of two types: operations scheduling and job scheduling. Job scheduling breaks the process down into individual job tasks with specific dates and times. It also designates the path along which the work will travel and the work centers that will be utilized.

21. A: The correct answer is "a," as the operations schedule is a longer-term plan, which assigns specific start and end dates to production orders. It is job scheduling that breaks the manufacture down into production stages and designates the work centers to be used. Most job scheduling for large-scale manufacture is done by computer and makes use of proximity of materials to work centers and availability of labor personnel. While operations scheduling takes a broad view of the manufacturing activity, job scheduling flexibility can result in leaner inventory and supply lines, as batch lots can often be broken down in further subdivision.

22. D: Answer "d" is the best choice—it is the only answer that embod.es all the processes; all of these manufacturing elements will cut down on bottlenecks, inventory bloat, and unresponsive manufacturing. In addition to the processes mentioned, synchronized manufacturing requires that all the manufacturing processes be synchronized and communicated throughout the system: prototyping and design validation; material movement and positioning; capacity management; demand forecasting; reporting, order tracking, and error management; and more. The alignment of all these processes involves a high level of coordination and collaboration between operational levels.

23. A: The correct answer is "a." Throughput efficiency of the utmost importance in the master planning process and higher rates of throughput efficiency can be obtained by reducing excessive setup and changeover times, by better integrated order processing schedules, and by improved communication along the pipeline as products move from end to end in the manufacturing stages. It is important that every step or stage in the manufacturing process add value to the product being manufactured; bottlenecks and a lack of visibility in the supply chain contribute to a large part of wasted throughput time.

24. C: The correct answer is "c," as the BOM (bill of materials) requires that components be listed as single items. Within this context, a "component" is the same thing as a subassembly. The subassembly must be entered as a single item because the computer software links the parent level with the component, which may consist of many smaller parts. In the auto industry, modular bills of materials assist in planning because the demand for the entire subassembly is as important an indicator of demand as seasonal annual sales figures.

25. C: The correct answer is "c." The two levels of materials requirements planning output are designated simply as Output 1 and Output 2. Output 1 refers to the recommended production schedule. The recommended production schedule creates a plan for quantities of material required and the minimal start and end dates for manufacturing production runs. The recommended purchasing schedule is aimed at the dates when the materials must arrive at the manufacturing facility.

26. B: Answer "b" has the correct answer. The first step is to construct a plan called the master production schedule, or MPS. From that point, the plan is subject to the MRP process, which computes materials demanded for manufacture of the product(s). Lot sizes are computed under the assumption that capacity is unlimited. The next step is capacity requirements planning, which further refines the manufacture by setting starting and ending times according to software algorithms. Capacity adjustment is nearly always needed, even at this point. The final step in the process is production control when production orders are released and ordering begins.

27. C: Answer "c" is correct because enterprise resource planning (ERP) is the latest development in a stage of manufacturing evolution that streamlined the production process through lean inventory management and technology. Machinery, personnel, financial resources, and software are integrated to make the manufacturing process function as a whole, with compatibility between systems a primary goal of ERP. All applications are derived from a single database, reducing costs and inefficiency by eliminating the need for expensive, independent standing information technology systems. ERP was first employed in the early 1990s.

28. B: The correct answer is "b." Cost management is a significant aspect for both manufacturing planning and manufacturing process control. The most common use of cost management is within the context of accounting and auditing functions, but it is also allied with management in decision making. During the master planning process, cost management software makes comparison of planned costs against actual costs, to project the impact of flexible options in manufacturing products or families of products.

29. A: Answer "a" is the correct answer. Master planning establishes a general map of all manufacturing activity associated with the production of a particular product or family of products. However, this ideal plan rarely conforms to the rigorous test of real world conditions in manufacturing. FMEA means Failure Mode and Effects Analysis, a process that analyzes the mathematical probabilities of failure in each phase of manufacturing. FMEA attempts to determine the severity of cost overruns and equipment failure and its impact on other phases of the manufacturing process.

30. D: The correct answer is "d"; all of the answer choices can impact manufacturing planning and should be part of the speculative scenarios of the master planning schedule. The objective of planning is to ensure profitability and develop effective reactive strategies to supply chain interruptions that may be caused by political or economic instability in supplier countries. The cost of commodities should be integrated into the planning process, inasmuch as resource planning requires the participation of financial resource components of manufacturing. It is common to factor in the price of energy, but the cost of other commodities can be a major factor in the success of some industries.

31. B: The best answer for this question is in answer "b." "All of the above" doesn't apply because "buying commodity options" protection will not help a company that needs to buy auto transmission assemblies from Mexico or Canada. The choice is essentially one of deciding whether to obtain material or components from a single supplier or from a wider variety of supplier options. The single materials supplier has communication and transportation advantages, but only if that supplier is inordinately stable. The question raises the issue of instability in the supplier country/countries so it would be best to develop relationships with multiple suppliers.

32. A: The best answer is "a," but all answer options may contribute to an understanding of why financial departments must be integrated into supply chain planning. In the case of "d," the cooking utensil inventory oversupply is simply a problem of poor inventory management planning. The auto manufacturer has a long-term contract, and the auto wheels must be provided at the expense of the supplier, so commodity price risk is not a factor for it. The aluminum foil manufacturer has wisely incorporated its financial arm to hedge its commodity position in a vital material. The aluminum door and window maker is at risk because the cost of its on-hand raw materials inventory may be noncompetitive at a time of severely decreased aluminum prices, such as we have now.

33. D: The correct answer is "d," and aluminum prices are on a drastic downtrend owing to an oversupply. When materials prices for a required manufacturing material are volatile, the control of inventory is imperative to ensure profitability. When future prices for aluminum deteriorate, the value of existing raw material aluminum stocks diminishes. Companies protect themselves by keeping inventories lean and by buying and selling short- and long-term aluminum positions that can move up or down.

34. D: The correct answer is "d" because the process of demand management requires all of the techniques required to fulfill demand. Beginning with the recognition of demand patterns, the process of demand management proceeds through forecasting changes in demand caused by seasonal or supply factors, and also includes order entry and order promising. Special attention must be given to the requirements of external warehousing and to the ordering of service parts between plant locations.

35. C: The correct answer is "c." To answer this question, it would help to know that AIDC stands for Auto ID Data Capture, for then you could conclude that inventory storage and movement data could be captured with bar code scanners and radio frequency identification devices. AIDC may also employ wireless local area networks and mobile computers that do more than read bar codes. Of course, the overall purpose is to monitor and process the movement and storage of inventory materials and related transactions like shipping, receiving, put away, and picking.

36. B: The correct answer is "b," the top management planning level. The question pertains to the fact that manufacturing planning and control, termed MPC, occurs at three distinct strategic levels: top management planning; operations management planning; and operations management execution. Top management planning includes sales and operation planning and also sets the resource requirements plan. During this phase of operations, managers set time frames for starting and completion and volume requirement levels by product group.

37. A: The correct answer is "a," since scheduling and capacity requirements planning is done at the operations management planning level. The question pertains to the fact that manufacturing planning and control, termed MPC, occurs at three distinct strategic levels: top management planning; operations management planning; and operations management execution. Capacity testing is also done at the operations management planning level to determine whether or not the master planning schedule sets attainable production goals.

38. D: The correct answer is "d." Safety stock levels can be easily set when historical demand is at well-known levels. A popular product or family of products, with a consistent demand curve allows inventory planners to set aside a reasonably accurate amount of safety stock. With new products, or products that are to be phased out, demand is far less predictable and the planning managers must set a fixed number or amount regardless of demand variation, usage, or supplier reliability. The fixed safety stock amount for a product being phased out can be set to zero.

39. B: Answer "b" is correct because it contains the formula for calculating time period safety stock. The time period method of calculating safety stock is most often used when supplier shipments are unpredictable and unreliable. The time periods of manufacture are broken down into time segments based on the quantity of parts necessary to meet demand during a known and predetermined time period. The calculation for time period safety stock can be represented as:

$SS = F \times T$, where SS represents safety stock; F is forecast usage; and T is the length of time for which the safety stock manufacturing segment is to be calculated.

40. D: The correct answer "d," because all of the answer options are ways of adjusting production capacity so. It is important to adhere to capacity requirements, so adjustments are often necessary. The inclusion or exclusion of work centers can be planned in advance to deal with demand fluctuations; moreover, workers can be added when required or assigned to other tasks when less capacity is warranted. The rescheduling of manufacturing orders is yet another way of adjusting capacity.

41. C: The correct answer is "c." The amount of available employee hours is obtained by subtracting the amount of employee hours used for released manufacturing orders from total available hours. Capacity resource planning software breaks employee hours down into three categories: employee hours used for released manufacturing orders; available employee hours remaining; and the %age of employee capacity used for released manufacturing orders.

42. C: Answer "c" is correct; post-operation time refers essentially to a waiting period observed before a product moves to the next manufacturing step. Post-operation time must be factored into processes that require it, such as when heated parts must be cooled, painted products must be allowed to dry, or materials like ceramics must be allowed to "cure." Not all processes require planners to factor in post-operation time; some products can move immediately to the next phase of manufacturing.

43. D: Correct answer is "d." A manufacturing instruction contains detailed work process information for workers processing parts. While general information for processing and handling can be contained on the routing sheet, manufacturing instructions are required for more complex and detailed processes. When additional and complex processes are required for unfinished inventory moving through a single line flow shop, there may not be a routing sheet (since all work moves the same way). In such cases, manufacturing instructions are absolutely necessary.

44. D: The best answer is "d"; it is also the most complete answer. Work center data are a vital part of ERP because it offers critical intelligence to future planning and design in future manufacturing. Work center data monitor and include such things as MTBF, employee and machine operating hours, and in evolved ERP systems, the information can be dispersed and integrated with customer demand on one end and with supplier inventory on the other.

45. B: The correct answer is "b." Fashion is a consumer-driven business with a short life cycle. The volatility can be explained by seasonal changes, by changing public tastes, by celebrity modeling, and by the impact of advertising. In materials planning, the product life cycle is an important consideration, impacting purchasing of raw materials and the assignment of materials to work centers. The volatility of the fashion industry can spread volatility to some parts of the commodities production industry—in cotton textiles, for example. Commodities have a longer life cycle, however, as do manufactured products in the auto industry and in industries producing large engineered products.

46. A: The best answer is "a." The layout of a work center is a vital part of manufacturing planning, and the major consideration determining what type of factory layout should be used is the type of product to be manufactured. The type of manufacturing mentioned in choice "d" is not a good choice and, in fact, must employ a "project layout" to be effectively accomplished. The cellular layout functions as a single unit with regard to work center files and routing sheets. Cellular layouts are a good choice for producing high-volume, low-variability products.

47. D: The correct answer is "d." Process planning for a cellular layout would require planners to determine the type of equipment most suitable to the manufacture and provide estimates of setup times, labor requirements, and time required for assembly. These components are all part of "process." Demand forecasting is part of selecting the product to be manufactured, so that eliminates answer "c" if MRO does not. MRO refers to maintenance, repair, and operating expenses—hardly a part of process engineering.

48. C: Answer "c" is the correct choice. Operations management planning is a midlevel MPC activity that entails all of the "nuts and bolts" of factory production steps that follow the general business, financing, and sales plans. RCCP is needed to establish maximum production capacity and the maximum levels of material and labor needed to support manufacturing. The master production schedule sets start and stop periods for various stages of manufacture. MRP sets the stage for the production schedule. Distribution planning ensures that all materials will be on hand to meet production schedules.

49. A: The correct answer is "a." The master schedule horizon represents the length of future time covered by the master schedule. The master schedule horizon must be long enough to allow time for ordering materials and manufacturing products. The master schedule horizon is divided into separate time periods consisting of the final assembly stage, the manufacturing and purchasing stage, and the look-ahead period. It is true that, as suggested in "b," time fences are (in addition to rough-cut capacity planning, or RCCP) used to test the feasibility of the master production schedule, but the question asks you to define the master schedule horizon.

How to Overcome Test Anxiety

Just the thought of taking a test is enough to make most people a little nervous. A test is an important event that can have a long-term impact on your future, so it's important to take it seriously and it's natural to feel anxious about performing well. But just because anxiety is normal, that doesn't mean that it's helpful in test taking, or that you should simply accept it as part of your life. Anxiety can have a variety of effects. These effects can be mild, like making you feel slightly nervous, or severe, like blocking your ability to focus or remember even a simple detail.

If you experience test anxiety—whether severe or mild—it's important to know how to beat it. To discover this, first you need to understand what causes test anxiety.

Causes of Test Anxiety

While we often think of anxiety as an uncontrollable emotional state, it can actually be caused by simple, practical things. One of the most common causes of test anxiety is that a person does not feel adequately prepared for their test. This feeling can be the result of many different issues such as poor study habits or lack of organization, but the most common culprit is time management. Starting to study too late, failing to organize your study time to cover all of the material, or being distracted while you study will mean that you're not well prepared for the test. This may lead to cramming the night before, which will cause you to be physically and mentally exhausted for the test. Poor time management also contributes to feelings of stress, fear, and hopelessness as you realize you are not well prepared but don't know what to do about it.

Other times, test anxiety is not related to your preparation for the test but comes from unresolved fear. This may be a past failure on a test, or poor performance on tests in general. It may come from comparing yourself to others who seem to be performing better or from the stress of living up to expectations. Anxiety may be driven by fears of the future—how failure on this test would affect your educational and career goals. These fears are often completely irrational, but they can still negatively impact your test performance.

Elements of Test Anxiety

As mentioned earlier, test anxiety is considered to be an emotional state, but it has physical and mental components as well. Sometimes you may not even realize that you are suffering from test anxiety until you notice the physical symptoms. These can include trembling hands, rapid heartbeat, sweating, nausea, and tense muscles. Extreme anxiety may lead to fainting or vomiting. Obviously, any of these symptoms can have a negative impact on testing. It is important to recognize them as soon as they begin to occur so that you can address the problem before it damages your performance.

The mental components of test anxiety include trouble focusing and inability to remember learned information. During a test, your mind is on high alert, which can help you recall information and stay focused for an extended period of time. However, anxiety interferes with your mind's natural processes, causing you to blank out, even on the questions you know well. The strain of testing during anxiety makes it difficult to stay focused, especially on a test that may take several hours. Extreme anxiety can take a huge mental toll, making it difficult not only to recall test information but even to understand the test questions or pull your thoughts together.

Effects of Test Anxiety

Test anxiety is like a disease—if left untreated, it will get progressively worse. Anxiety leads to poor performance, and this reinforces the feelings of fear and failure, which in turn lead to poor performances on subsequent tests. It can grow from a mild nervousness to a crippling condition. If allowed to progress, test anxiety can have a big impact on your schooling, and consequently on your future.

Test anxiety can spread to other parts of your life. Anxiety on tests can become anxiety in any stressful situation, and blanking on a test can turn into panicking in a job situation. But fortunately, you don't have to let anxiety rule your testing and determine your grades. There are a number of relatively simple steps you can take to move past anxiety and function normally on a test and in the rest of life.

Physical Steps for Beating Test Anxiety

While test anxiety is a serious problem, the good news is that it can be overcome. It doesn't have to control your ability to think and remember information. While it may take time, you can begin taking steps today to beat anxiety.

Just as your first hint that you may be struggling with anxiety comes from the physical symptoms, the first step to treating it is also physical. Rest is crucial for having a clear, strong mind. If you are tired, it is much easier to give in to anxiety. But if you establish good sleep habits, your body and mind will be ready to perform optimally, without the strain of exhaustion. Additionally, sleeping well helps you to retain information better, so you're more likely to recall the answers when you see the test questions.

Getting good sleep means more than going to bed on time. It's important to allow your brain time to relax. Take study breaks from time to time so it doesn't get overworked, and don't study right before bed. Take time to rest your mind before trying to rest your body, or you may find it difficult to fall asleep.

Along with sleep, other aspects of physical health are important in preparing for a test. Good nutrition is vital for good brain function. Sugary foods and drinks may give a burst of energy but this burst is followed by a crash, both physically and emotionally. Instead, fuel your body with protein and vitamin-rich foods.

Also, drink plenty of water. Dehydration can lead to headaches and exhaustion, especially if your brain is already under stress from the rigors of the test. Particularly if your test is a long one, drink water during the breaks. And if possible, take an energy-boosting snack to eat between sections.

Along with sleep and diet, a third important part of physical health is exercise. Maintaining a steady workout schedule is helpful, but even taking 5-minute study breaks to walk can help get your blood pumping faster and clear your head. Exercise also releases endorphins, which contribute to a positive feeling and can help combat test anxiety.

When you nurture your physical health, you are also contributing to your mental health. If your body is healthy, your mind is much more likely to be healthy as well. So take time to rest, nourish your body with healthy food and water, and get moving as much as possible. Taking these physical steps will make you stronger and more able to take the mental steps necessary to overcome test anxiety.

Mental Steps for Beating Test Anxiety

Working on the mental side of test anxiety can be more challenging, but as with the physical side, there are clear steps you can take to overcome it. As mentioned earlier, test anxiety often stems from lack of preparation, so the obvious solution is to prepare for the test. Effective studying may be the most important weapon you have for beating test anxiety, but you can and should employ several other mental tools to combat fear.

First, boost your confidence by reminding yourself of past success—tests or projects that you aced. If you're putting as much effort into preparing for this test as you did for those, there's no reason you should expect to fail here. Work hard to prepare; then trust your preparation.

Second, surround yourself with encouraging people. It can be helpful to find a study group, but be sure that the people you're around will encourage a positive attitude. If you spend time with others who are anxious or cynical, this will only contribute to your own anxiety. Look for others who are motivated to study hard from a desire to succeed, not from a fear of failure.

Third, reward yourself. A test is physically and mentally tiring, even without anxiety, and it can be helpful to have something to look forward to. Plan an activity following the test, regardless of the outcome, such as going to a movie or getting ice cream.

When you are taking the test, if you find yourself beginning to feel anxious, remind yourself that you know the material. Visualize successfully completing the test. Then take a few deep, relaxing breaths and return to it. Work through the questions carefully but with confidence, knowing that you are capable of succeeding.

Developing a healthy mental approach to test taking will also aid in other areas of life. Test anxiety affects more than just the actual test—it can be damaging to your mental health and even contribute to depression. It's important to beat test anxiety before it becomes a problem for more than testing.

Study Strategy

Being prepared for the test is necessary to combat anxiety, but what does being prepared look like? You may study for hours on end and still not feel prepared. What you need is a strategy for test prep. The next few pages outline our recommended steps to help you plan out and conquer the challenge of preparation.

Step 1: Scope Out the Test

Learn everything you can about the format (multiple choice, essay, etc.) and what will be on the test. Gather any study materials, course outlines, or sample exams that may be available. Not only will this help you to prepare, but knowing what to expect can help to alleviate test anxiety.

Step 2: Map Out the Material

Look through the textbook or study guide and make note of how many chapters or sections it has. Then divide these over the time you have. For example, if a book has 15 chapters and you have five days to study, you need to cover three chapters each day. Even better, if you have the time, leave an extra day at the end for overall review after you have gone through the material in depth.

If time is limited, you may need to prioritize the material. Look through it and make note of which sections you think you already have a good grasp on, and which need review. While you are studying, skim quickly through the familiar sections and take more time on the challenging parts.

Write out your plan so you don't get lost as you go. Having a written plan also helps you feel more in control of the study, so anxiety is less likely to arise from feeling overwhelmed at the amount to cover.

Step 3: Gather Your Tools

Decide what study method works best for you. Do you prefer to highlight in the book as you study and then go back over the highlighted portions? Or do you type out notes of the important information? Or is it helpful to make flashcards that you can carry with you? Assemble the pens, index cards, highlighters, post-it notes, and any other materials you may need so you won't be distracted by getting up to find things while you study.

If you're having a hard time retaining the information or organizing your notes, experiment with different methods. For example, try color-coding by subject with colored pens, highlighters, or post-it notes. If you learn better by hearing, try recording yourself reading your notes so you can listen while in the car, working out, or simply sitting at your desk. Ask a friend to quiz you from your flashcards, or try teaching someone the material to solidify it in your mind.

Step 4: Create Your Environment

It's important to avoid distractions while you study. This includes both the obvious distractions like visitors and the subtle distractions like an uncomfortable chair (or a too-comfortable couch that makes you want to fall asleep). Set up the best study environment possible: good lighting and a comfortable work area. If background music helps you focus, you may want to turn it on, but otherwise keep the room quiet. If you are using a computer to take notes, be sure you don't have any other windows open, especially applications like social media, games, or anything else that could distract you. Silence your phone and turn off notifications. Be sure to keep water close by so you stay hydrated while you study (but avoid unhealthy drinks and snacks).

Also, take into account the best time of day to study. Are you freshest first thing in the morning? Try to set aside some time then to work through the material. Is your mind clearer in the afternoon or evening? Schedule your study session then. Another method is to study at the same time of day that you will take the test, so that your brain gets used to working on the material at that time and will be ready to focus at test time.

Step 5: Study!

Once you have done all the study preparation, it's time to settle into the actual studying. Sit down, take a few moments to settle your mind so you can focus, and begin to follow your study plan. Don't give in to distractions or let yourself procrastinate. This is your time to prepare so you'll be ready to fearlessly approach the test. Make the most of the time and stay focused.

Of course, you don't want to burn out. If you study too long you may find that you're not retaining the information very well. Take regular study breaks. For example, taking five minutes out of every hour to walk briskly, breathing deeply and swinging your arms, can help your mind stay fresh.

As you get to the end of each chapter or section, it's a good idea to do a quick review. Remind yourself of what you learned and work on any difficult parts. When you feel that you've mastered the material, move on to the next part. At the end of your study session, briefly skim through your notes again.

But while review is helpful, cramming last minute is NOT. If at all possible, work ahead so that you won't need to fit all your study into the last day. Cramming overloads your brain with more information than it can process and retain, and your tired mind may struggle to recall even previously learned information when it is overwhelmed with last-minute study. Also, the urgent nature of cramming and the stress placed on your brain contribute to anxiety. You'll be more likely to go to the test feeling unprepared and having trouble thinking clearly.

So don't cram, and don't stay up late before the test, even just to review your notes at a leisurely pace. Your brain needs rest more than it needs to go over the information again. In fact, plan to finish your studies by noon or early afternoon the day before the test. Give your brain the rest of the day to relax or focus on other things, and get a good night's sleep. Then you will be fresh for the test and better able to recall what you've studied.

Step 6: Take a Practice Test

Many courses offer sample tests, either online or in the study materials. This is an excellent resource to check whether you have mastered the material, as well as to prepare for the test format and environment.

Check the test format ahead of time: the number of questions, the type (multiple choice, free response, etc.), and the time limit. Then create a plan for working through them. For example, if you have 30 minutes to take a 60-question test, your limit is 30 seconds per question. Spend less time on the questions you know well so that you can take more time on the difficult ones.

If you have time to take several practice tests, take the first one open book, with no time limit. Work through the questions at your own pace and make sure you fully understand them. Gradually work up to taking a test under test conditions: sit at a desk with all study materials put away and set a timer. Pace yourself to make sure you finish the test with time to spare and go back to check your answers if you have time.

After each test, check your answers. On the questions you missed, be sure you understand why you missed them. Did you misread the question (tests can use tricky wording)? Did you forget the information? Or was it something you hadn't learned? Go back and study any shaky areas that the practice tests reveal.

Taking these tests not only helps with your grade, but also aids in combating test anxiety. If you're already used to the test conditions, you're less likely to worry about it, and working through tests until you're scoring well gives you a confidence boost. Go through the practice tests until you feel comfortable, and then you can go into the test knowing that you're ready for it.

Test Tips

On test day, you should be confident, knowing that you've prepared well and are ready to answer the questions. But aside from preparation, there are several test day strategies you can employ to maximize your performance.

First, as stated before, get a good night's sleep the night before the test (and for several nights before that, if possible). Go into the test with a fresh, alert mind rather than staying up late to study.

Try not to change too much about your normal routine on the day of the test. It's important to eat a nutritious breakfast, but if you normally don't eat breakfast at all, consider eating just a protein bar. If you're a coffee drinker, go ahead and have your normal coffee. Just make sure you time it so that the caffeine doesn't wear off right in the middle of your test. Avoid sugary beverages, and drink enough water to stay hydrated but not so much that you need a restroom break 10 minutes into the test. If your test isn't first thing in the morning, consider going for a walk or doing a light workout before the test to get your blood flowing.

Allow yourself enough time to get ready, and leave for the test with plenty of time to spare so you won't have the anxiety of scrambling to arrive in time. Another reason to be early is to select a good seat. It's helpful to sit away from doors and windows, which can be distracting. Find a good seat, get out your supplies, and settle your mind before the test begins.

When the test begins, start by going over the instructions carefully, even if you already know what to expect. Make sure you avoid any careless mistakes by following the directions.

Then begin working through the questions, pacing yourself as you've practiced. If you're not sure on an answer, don't spend too much time on it, and don't let it shake your confidence. Either skip it and come back later, or eliminate as many wrong answers as possible and guess among the remaining ones. Don't dwell on these questions as you continue—put them out of your mind and focus on what lies ahead.

Be sure to read all of the answer choices, even if you're sure the first one is the right answer. Sometimes you'll find a better one if you keep reading. But don't second-guess yourself if you do immediately know the answer. Your gut instinct is usually right. Don't let test anxiety rob you of the information you know.

If you have time at the end of the test (and if the test format allows), go back and review your answers. Be cautious about changing any, since your first instinct tends to be correct, but make sure you didn't misread any of the questions or accidentally mark the wrong answer choice. Look over any you skipped and make an educated guess.

At the end, leave the test feeling confident. You've done your best, so don't waste time worrying about your performance or wishing you could change anything. Instead, celebrate the successful completion of this test. And finally, use this test to learn how to deal with anxiety even better next time.

Review Video: Test Anxiety
Visit mometrix.com/academy and enter code: 100340

Important Qualification

Not all anxiety is created equal. If your test anxiety is causing major issues in your life beyond the classroom or testing center, or if you are experiencing troubling physical symptoms related to your anxiety, it may be a sign of a serious physiological or psychological condition. If this sounds like your situation, we strongly encourage you to seek professional help.

Online Resources

Due to our efforts to try to keep this book to a manageable length, we've created a link that will give you access to all of your online resources:

mometrix.com/resources719/cpimmpr

It's Your Moment, Let's Celebrate It!

Share your story @mometrixtestpreparation